Civil Procedure in Denmark

Civil Procedure in Denmark

Fourth Edition

Lars Lindencrone Petersen

This book was originally published as a monograph in the International Encyclopaedia of Laws/Civil Procedure.

Wolters Kluwer

Published by:
Kluwer Law International B.V.
PO Box 316
2400 AH Alphen aan den Rijn
The Netherlands
E-mail: lrs-sales@wolterskluwer.com
Website: www.wolterskluwer.com/en/solutions/kluwerlawinternational

Sold and distributed by:
Wolters Kluwer Legal & Regulatory U.S.
7201 McKinney Circle
Frederick, MD 21704
United States of America
E-mail: customer.service@wolterskluwer.com

ISBN 978-94-035-0196-3

e-Book: ISBN 978-94-035-0376-9
web-PDF: ISBN 978-94-035-0386-8

The Author

Lars Lindencrone Petersen served as a judge in the City Court of Copenhagen, the Maritime and Commercial Court and the High Court for Eastern Denmark for seventeen years before, in 2008, he joined Bech-Bruun Law Firm as a partner.

He has been chairman of several expert committees preparing legislative amendments, including the Act of Insurance Agreements and the rules on Floating Charge and has been chairman of the Bankruptcy Council (a standing expert committee advising the Danish government on insolvency law matters).

He has extensive experience as an arbitrator in ad hoc, institutional and labour law-based cases.

He has written numerous books on procedural law, enterprise law in general and insolvency law in particular.

As of 2011, he is an adjunct professor at the Faculty of Law at Aarhus University, Denmark.

The Author

Table of Contents

List of Abbreviations

AA	Danish Arbitration Act 2005
ADR	Alternative Dispute Resolution
CFI	Court of First Instance (Luxembourg)
ECHR	European Court of Human Rights (Strasbourg)
ECJ	European Court of Justice (Luxembourg)
EEA	European Economic Area
EHRC	European Human Rights Convention
EU	European Union
H	*Højesteret* (Danish Supreme Court Judgment or Decision)
ICC	International Court of Arbitration
J	*Juristen* (the Danish journal; the Lawyer)
LCIA	London Court of International Arbitration
PIL	Private International Law
R	*Rigsretten* (The Danish Special Court for Impeachment Cases)
Rpl	*Retsplejeloven* (The Danish Administration of Justice Act)
S.U.	*Skat Udland* (The Danish Tax Journal)
SvJT	*Svensk Juristtidning* (The Swedish Law Journal)
TFA	*Tidsskrift for Familie- og Arveret* (The Danish Journal)
TfR	*Tidsskrift for Rettsvitenskap* (The Nordic Journal)
TfS	*Tidsskrift for Skatter og Afgifter* (The Danish Journal)
UfR	*Ugeskrift for Retsvæsen* (The Danish Journal)
UNCITRAL	United Nations Commission on International Trade Law
V	*Vestre Landsret* (Danish Western High Court Judgment or Decision)
Ø	*Østre Landsret* (Danish Eastern High Court Judgment or Decision)

List of Abbreviations

General Introduction

§1. General Background

1. Denmark is a kingdom comprising the territory of Denmark plus Greenland and the Faroe Islands. Both Greenland and the Faroe Islands have considerable autonomy within the kingdom.

The government, as described in section 1 of the Constitution of 1953 (*Danmarks Riges Grundlov*, or simply: *Grundloven*), is a 'limited monarchy'.

The 1953 Constitution is based on Denmark's first constitution of 1849, which ended the absolute monarchy and introduced democracy. Cabinet responsibility was recognized in 1901 and is now laid down in section 15 of the Constitution, under which no minister can remain in office after Parliament (*Folketinget*) has expressed its lack of confidence in him.

2. Denmark has no constitutional court, and establishment of such a court would require a constitutional amendment. The question of whether Parliament respects the Constitution and, for that matter, its obligations under the European Union law (EU law), the European Human Rights Convention (EHRC), etc., is therefore a matter for the ordinary courts, and in final instance, the Supreme Court. There is no court with the competence to make a hypothetical evaluation in advance of whether any particular Act is compatible with the Constitution, and there is no general right of the individual citizen to take legal action (*actio popularis*).

The compatibility of a piece of legislation with the Constitution can therefore only be tested by a citizen or a company who or which is specifically affected by the question.[1]

3. Public access to and oral proceedings in the courts must be ensured 'to the greatest possible extent' (cf. section 65, subsection 1 of the Constitution), and laymen (lay assessors and jurors) must take part in criminal procedure (cf. section 65, subsection 2), but the extent of such participation is not further specified. The Court Reform 2007/2008 actualized questions of the interpretation of section 65, subsection 2, because it is part of the reform that jury cases (as a main rule: criminal cases where at least four years in prison is at stake) must start in the local city court with

1. However, in the case of Denmark's accession to the EU Treaty, the Supreme Court has – in contrast to its previous practice – stretched the right of action (the concept of 'cause of action') a long way (cf. *UfR* 1996:1300 H). The Supreme Court appears in this case to have been inspired by the right of action possessed by citizens of other countries with respect to the constitutionality of law.

three professional judges and a jury of six, and the professional judges as well as the jurors must deliberate and vote together, instead of voting separated from each other. Part of the jurisprudence claimed that this might be contrary to section 65, subsection 2, but the reform was adopted nevertheless, and it seems to function well.

4. With effect from 2007/2008, a major reform of the Danish administration of justice, both civil and criminal, as well as reform of the courts themselves (*the Court Reform 2007/2008*) was adopted by Parliament on suggestion from the Danish Civil Justice Council (*Retsplejerådet*).

Civil administration of justice in Denmark was under major pressure from a number of sides: commercial companies often prefer arbitration in place of a court case, notwithstanding the fact that arbitration is typically more expensive and also involves renunciation of a fundamental legal right, the right to appeal. In administrative cases, it is often not the courts but the boards of appeal which are asked to review the case, partly because they are highly specialized and partly because a complaint to them is normally far cheaper than a court case.

The judicial system was often not used in debt collection cases because, rightly or wrongly, it is thought to be slow and expensive, and debt collection agencies or the 'grey market' are used instead.

Recognizing that the courts should be re-established as the pivotal venue for the resolution of disputes, the Court Reform 2007/2008 attempted to streamline the Danish courts in order to make them more 'competitive' compared to arbitration, various appeal boards, etc., through the following ways:

- The number of court districts was cut down from eighty-two to twenty-four, thus allowing the courts to operate in larger units, and allowing the judges to specialize.
- A cheaper small claims procedure, with a more active and investigating part to play for the court than in normal civil proceedings, was introduced (for demands up to DKK 50,000, corresponding to approximately EUR 6,700).
- A fast track procedure was introduced for claims which are not contested, but which are nevertheless still not fulfilled.
- The concept of class actions was introduced in Danish law.
- Cases are tried in the first instance by the city court, no matter what is the size of the claim (however, with the option of referring civil cases concerning fundamental issues to the High Court as first instance court).
- The Maritime and Commercial Court is concentrated on some specialized fields of law, including commercial cases with international aspects (where the international aspect can just be the parties' domicile in different countries).

§2. Delimitation of the Subject Matter

I. Definition of the Term 'Civil Procedure'

5. Danish civil proceedings or, in the words of the Administration of Justice Act (*Retsplejeloven* – Rpl), the 'civil procedure' comprise cases between private citizens, companies, public authorities, etc., which are not criminal cases.

Danish civil proceedings are thus best defined in negative terms. They are not restricted to traditional disputes where one party is demanding money from another party (or claiming that a party should stop a particular activity, acknowledge a property right, etc.); they also include special proceedings in cases involving matrimonial matters and custody of children, paternity, guardianship, the testing of detention by administrative decision (e.g., under psychiatric care legislation) and cancellation, and property title cases.

II. Distinction with Other Types of Procedure

6. Civil procedure must always be kept separate from the administration, i.e., from administrative authorities (cf. section 62 of the Constitution). The courts can always test administrative Acts (cf. section 63 of the Constitution, which, however, also prescribes that taking the administrative Acts to the courts does not stay the execution). Under the influence of the decision by the European Court in *Factortame* I,[2] the Supreme Court in *Gyproc A/S* deemed that this constitutional clause did not bar the courts from granting a stay of execution in connection with proceedings involving an administrative Act.[3] Further reform was introduced with effect from 1 July 2013, reshaping all the provisions on interim measures. The reform has, as the main rule, moved the competence in such interim measures from the bailiff's court to the court that has to treat the substance of the case.

7. Section 63 of the Constitution provides the scope for establishing one or more separate administrative courts, provided that their decisions can be appealed to the Supreme Court. No use has been made of this provision, and there are at present no actual plans to do so, although one of the items which the Danish Civil Justice Council (*Retsplejerådet*) is going to examine closer is the possibility of shaping a special kind of process, with or without special administrative courts, for administrative cases.

The function exercised by administrative courts in some countries is largely filled in Denmark by complaints boards structured very similarly to courts, often with a judge presiding (one might call them: 'small and specialized discount administrative courts'. This is not a fair expression because they are often highly specialized and competent), and also filled by the parliamentary Ombudsman (*Folketingets Ombudsmand*, or simply: *Ombudsmanden*, not to be confused with the Consumer Ombudsman, *Forbrugerombudsmanden*), whose constitutional responsibility under

2. C-213/89.
3. Cf. *UfR* 1994:823 H.

section 55 is to 'superintend the state's civil and military administration', i.e., a broad competence to check whether public authorities are committing any error or negligence in the performance of their administrative duties.

The Ombudsman's independence is beyond question, and he and his decisions enjoy considerable respect. He steps into action upon receiving a complaint, or ex officio. He can either attend to individual cases or perform a more general testing of the administrative practices of a particular authority, including 'systemic errors', etc.

It was the Ombudsman's investigations into, and heavy criticism against, the government's practice in some foreigner's cases (now herostratically known in Denmark as *the Tamil* case) that led in 1993 to the fall of the conservative-liberal government responsible for deliberately delaying the cases of the Tamil refugees. The Ombudsman's criticism led to a long and profound investigation conducted by Supreme Court justice Mogens Hornslet, giving its conclusions in January 1993. Hours after the Commission's conclusions, the government resigned. The painful end of the case was, for the first time in almost a century, an impeachment against the Minister of Justice responsible for the Tamil case, Mr Erik Ninn-Hansen. The Special Court for Impeachment (*Rigsretten*) found Mr Ninn-Hansen guilty and sentenced him to some months in prison, however a suspended sentence.[4]

III. Separate Court Systems and Rules of Procedure

8. In Denmark, civil and criminal cases are decided by the same courts, i.e., there are no specialized criminal courts. Just as with civil cases, criminal cases start in the city court as first instance, no matter whether the criminal case is presided by only one professional judge (small cases where no imprisonment is at stake), or by one professional judge and two lay judges (more serious cases where imprisonment under four years is at stake), or by three professional judges and six jurors (serious cases where imprisonment of four years or more is at stake) (the four-year limit is not without exceptions; for example, cases of economic crime are always heard by one professional judge and two lay judges).

Criminal cases may also, with 'permission of third instance' from the Appeals Permission Board (*Procesbevillingsnævnet*), be heard by the Supreme Court, but because no laymen are sitting in the Supreme Court (neither lay judges nor jurors), its competence in criminal cases is limited. The Supreme Court can only test whether the provisions criminalizing the behaviour (in the Criminal Code or special Act) are correctly interpreted, whether the sentence is meted out correctly and whether the case was fairly heard in the lower courts. The Supreme Court cannot, however, test the evidence (the facts of the case), but must base its decision on the assessment of evidence performed by the High Court.

Thus, it is a misunderstanding when newspapers often write that 'the Supreme Court cannot test the question of guilt'. It certainly can, as far as this test is based on assessing *the law*, not on assessing *the facts* of the case. A number of cases can be demonstrated where lower instances found the accused guilty, but the Supreme

4. Cf. *UfR* 1994:409 R.

Court interpreted the relevant *jus* in such a way that the accused was acquitted. The Supreme Court will even do this ex officio.[5] Thus, e.g., the Supreme Court annulled the judgment regarding an accountant who, on his confession had been convicted for participation in his client's tax fraud. The Supreme Court did not find that the relevant tax provisions provided the necessary legal basis for convicting him, and thus the judgments of the city court and the High Court, even in this confession case, were annulled by the Supreme Court, and the case referred back to the lower courts.

9. Basically, the same procedural provisions, the *Rpl*, apply to both civil and criminal cases, and a number of provisions in the *Rpl* are the same for both types of cases, for example, the rules on witnesses, deliberation and consideration, etc. However, the Act also contains chapters relating specifically to civil or criminal cases.

The main difference is that:

- *civil cases* are, like most other countries, governed largely by the principle that the parties themselves define the issue, claims and arguments of the case, and the principle that the parties are free to dispose of the subject matter of the case regardless of the action pending; i.e., the case is dispositive in nature; while
- *criminal cases* are, like most other countries, dominated by the principle of 'objective truth', under which the court must seek to establish what really happened.

The difference is, as was already the case under early Roman law, best illustrated in the importance of a confession in the two types of cases. In civil proceedings, a confession is *dispositive* in its effect. The court applies it untested. In criminal proceedings, a confession is only one piece of evidence among several, albeit, of course, an important one. The court must test whether the confession, together with other pieces of evidence, points to the guilt of the accused.

10. The *Rpl* does not contain all the rules governing Danish courts as the *Rpl* only applies to the ordinary courts listed below, paragraphs 31–34. One important institution not governed by the *Rpl* is the Labour Court (*Arbejdsretten*), which plays an important role in the settling of legal disputes under employment law, the constitution and function of which are set out in the Industrial Relations Act.

This Court hears cases on the breach and interpretation of general agreements and collective agreements, questions on the existence of collective agreements and the legality of hostile measures called or already applied. In areas where the Labour Court possesses sole competence, the case cannot be taken to the ordinary courts, not even by appeal. Ordinary questions of employment, such as a dispute between an employee and his (former) employer, are brought before the ordinary courts, i.e., the city court, with an appeal to the High Court.

5. Cf. *UfR* 1989:128 H.

§3. Sources of Civil Procedure Law

11. The primary means of regulating the administration of justice in Denmark is *Rpl*. This Act with its well over 1,000 sections came into being in the early twentieth century (1916), thus celebrating its 100th anniversary in 2016. It came into force at a time when large statute books were the fashion.

The Act has stood the distance well, and there are no plans to replace it with one or more other statutes. It is, however, regularly amended, and as mentioned above under paragraph 4, a major reform was adopted in 2007/2008, reducing the number of jurisdictions to twenty-four city courts, with fewer and larger city courts with better scope for specialization for lawyers, combined with a more rational procedure in civil cases, allowing the hearing (the oral hearing, the main trial) to be concentrated and condensed. The main scope of the reform has, as mentioned under paragraph 6, been to streamline the courts and make them 'competitive' in competition with arbitration, complaint boards, etc.

12. Denmark is very much aware of the obligations arising from the EHRC and its requirements concerning a fair trial, both in civil and criminal cases. These obligations are reflected not only in specific decisions, where *Rpl* provisions are complemented by EHRC considerations, but also in amendments to the *Rpl* aimed specifically at bringing it into compliance with the EHRC.

One of the numerous examples was the change in the *Rpl* rules on the impartiality of judges when, on 24 May 1989, a judgment was pronounced against Denmark in the European Court of Human Rights (ECHR) in the case of *Hauschildt v. Denmark*. Since the amendment, a judge who has detained an accused during the initial hearing of a criminal case on the basis of 'highly probable cause' (i.e., a high degree of likelihood that a criminal act has been committed) cannot subsequently judge the case on its merits. Thus, not only the city court where such verdicts on detainment have been pronounced, but also the Appeal Court (the Western or the Eastern Appeal Court, *Vestre Landsret* resp. *Østre Landsret*), having dealt with appeal cases on the question of detainment, thoroughly keeps lists of the judges who have participated in such detainment cases, in order to be sure that these judges do not at a later stage judge the case on its merits, neither in the first instance nor in the appeal stage.

An impact was also created when judgment was handed down against Denmark in the ECHR in the tragic cases of haemophiliacs who had received unscreened blood. The civil compensation case against the Danish State and a medical company had been underway far too long (cf. the court's judgment of 8 February 1996).

Recognizing that the waiting period for civil proceedings in Danish courts was a problem in light of the content of Article 6, subsection 1 of the EHRC, the *Rpl* provisions governing case preparation and the handing down of judgment, etc., were tightened in 1997. It is clear from the Preamble that one of the main motives behind the bill was the desire to ensure compliance with the EHRC's requirements regarding the right to have one's case decided within a 'reasonable time'. The general intention behind the changes was to strengthen formal case management considerably. The years that have passed since this amendment to the *Rpl* show very clearly that the courts have taken it seriously to speed up the cases.

Another example: It is well known that Article 11 ECHR guarantees not only the positive but also the negative freedom of association; you have the right to *be* a member of an association, but you also have the right *not* to be a member of that, or of any, association. When the ECHR decided, in a Danish case, that an employee cannot be forced to join a certain union (or to join a union at all), not even if he accepted such membership when obtaining his job, the Danish legislator took the full consequence of this judgment and decided that the *Advokatsamfundet* ('The Danish Bar and Law Society') cannot any longer be a union with forced membership for all practising lawyers, but can only act as an organ with disciplinary competences towards the practising lawyers.[6] And thus another independent organization, *Danske Advokater* ('The Association of Danish Law Firms'), was established in order to act as a union for those practising lawyers who *wish* to be members.

13. Important procedural rules are also found outside the *Rpl*, but such rules must always be supplemented and filled in by the rules of the *Rpl.* The Bankruptcy Act (*konkursloven*), the Administration of Estates of Deceased Persons Act (*dødsboskifteloven*) and the Lease Act on Real Estate (*lejeloven*) all contain a series of procedural rules for bankrupt estates, estates of deceased persons and disputes between owners and tenants. Special legislation may also contain procedural rules such as deadlines for taking legal action, for example, rules in the Tax Administration Act (*skatteforvaltningsloven*) on court action for testing decisions by the tax authorities, including the highest administrative tax instance, the National Tax Tribunal (*Landsskatteretten*), which is, in spite of its name, *not* a court, but an administrative organ.

§4. General Features of the Administration of Justice in Civil Matters

I. Characteristics of the Procedure

14. The procedure in civil cases is distinctly adversarial. The court does not conduct its investigations but relies on the fact and evidence placed before it by the parties. This principle, which Denmark of course shares with most other states, is in Danish called *forhandlingsmaksimen* or: *forhandlingsprincippet* (corresponding to German: *Verhandlungsprinzip*), i.e., the principle of party presentation (cf. *Rpl* section 338).

One of the points where the civil procedure is highly formal is with regard to the so-called procedural 'provocations' (requests for further and better particulars, *provokationer*). Unlike criminal cases, the object of the court is not to establish the absolute, objective truth, but rather a 'relative', 'subjective' truth on the basis of the materials which the parties themselves produce to the court in the form of claims, allegations and evidence. The idea behind this principle is, like in other countries, that the parties are those who know their own case best, and the parties must decide

6. *Sørensen & Rasmussen v. Denmark*, 11 Jan. 2006.

exactly how many resources they want to spend on the case. Therefore, it is the parties who define the framework of the case. Both parties must, therefore, give careful consideration to the question of what to produce in order to prove what actually took place. The civil procedure is also different from the administrative procedure in this respect, as the inquisitorial procedure places the burden of proof solely with the administrative authority (although the procedure before a number of appeal boards in administrative cases tends to be based on principles like the ones applied by the courts in civil matters, i.e., that the parties must provide the board with their claims, evidence and allegations).

15. Requests to the opposite party can, for example, occur in situations where one party presents its view of some aspect of the case and requests the other party to agree with this view. If the other party does agree, no evidence can or may be called for on the question, as the court must not admit superfluous or irrelevant evidence (cf. section 341). It is usually not the responsibility of the court to verify whether the facts really are as the parties claim.

If a party presents his case in an unclear or ambiguous manner, it may count against him in the court's assessment of what evidence should be applied in the case. The same applies if a party is silent on a matter unless he has already contested the point in question. If, for example, the plaintiff presents his view on a point of fact in the writ and requests the defendant to declare his agreement with this, but the defendant avoids the question in his statement of defence and does not return to it in any subsequent rejoinder, but then attempts to contest the point at the oral hearing, the court may then decide, if so requested by the plaintiff, to apply the evidence produced by the plaintiff in the writ.

This is the so-called prejudicial effect which we meet in many disguises in civil procedure. The court is not obliged to apply this sanction, but it must assess whether it should be applied. It is thus a facultative or optional sanction, and its full designation in Danish is therefore '*fakultativ processuel skadevirkning*'. If, for example, a company sues another company for plagiarizing a design, and the plaintiff requests the defendant to produce further and better particulars with regard to its own development work but this request is ignored, this may have a prejudicial effect on the defendant's case on the assumption that if the defendant fails to document his development work, it probably means that no development took place – which of course supports the plaintiff's claim of plagiarism.

16. If a party fails to fulfil a procedural request, the opponent who made the request may go even further and apply the *Rpl* rule on discovery (Danish: *edition*). This means that the court issues an order of discovery (*editionskendelse*) against the party (cf. sections 298 and 300). The decision whether to apply a sanction against the party on this ground is not made until the hearing and the preparation of judgment.[7] However, it has been established by the courts that a party cannot go 'fishing' for internal documents that may exist with the other party and that some documents are to remain – internal. In *Heini Joensen*, the Supreme Court refused to

7. Cf. *UfR* 1999:1475 Ø.

order Jyske Bank to produce some internal credit evaluations in a large case of disappointed investors.[8] In *Hafnia* on liability for stock prospectus and stock emission, Danske Bank was ordered to produce parts of its internal board minutes of deliberations, however, anonymized and extracted.[9]

Also, a third party who is not party to the case may be ordered by the court (also through an *editionskendelse*) to submit documents in his or her possession. An example is the various cases following the financial crisis and the collapse of banks where the board and management have been held responsible for the bank's losses, or where attempts have been made in order to hold them responsible. In such cases, the Danish Financial Supervision Authority (Danish: *Finanstilsynet* (FSA)) may very well be in possession of valuable documents showing what the Inspection knew, or did not know, about the bank that ended up in a collapse. On request from one of the defendants (the chairman of the bank's board of directors) in one of these bank cases, *Vestre Landsret* (the Western High Court) ordered the FSA to submit to the parties of the case, and to the High Court, every letter, email, note, etc., sent from the FSA to the bank during the years 2006–2008 (the years for which the board members as well as the management of the bank were allegedly liable for the bank's losses).[10]

17. One provision in the *Rpl*, which has already been mentioned, plays so crucial a role in the civil procedure (and only there) that it deserves to be cited in full (cf. *Rpl* section 338): 'The court cannot grant a party more than he has claimed and can only take into consideration such allegations as the party has made, or which cannot be withdrawn.'

In all its brevity, this is, as already mentioned, the principle of party presentation (*forhandlingsmaksimen*) – the court does not conduct its own investigations but relies on the fact and evidence placed before it by the parties. The principle does not mean that the parties themselves 'control' the hearings (this is, of course, the task of the court, as it is responsible for formal procedural management), but that the parties themselves decide what should be included in the hearings, and thus the framework within which the court must make its decision.

The counterpart to this principle is the principle of the inquisitorial procedure, where the courts (or the administrative authorities) are responsible for producing the evidence and investigating the case. This maxim is, for example, used in countries with separate administrative courts, where it is the responsibility of the courts to produce the requisite evidence in the case in order to reach the right substantive decision.

The principle of party presentation (*forhandlingsmaksimen*) includes both a party's claims and the party's allegations for his claims.

Example of the impact on the claim of the principle of party representation (*forhandlingsmaksimen*): If A raises a claim against B for DKK 100,000, but the court can see that A could actually have demanded DKK 120,000, it can still not

8. Cf. *UfR* 1999:1028 H.
9. Cf. *UfR* 2002:1734 H.
10. *See Vestre Landsret's* decision of 15 Oct. 2014 in case V.L. B-0427-11.

award A more than his claim: DKK 100,000. The court can in a discrete way exercise its right of asking questions, however never hereby leaving the court's duty of impartiality. If the questions do not cause A to raise his claim, then DKK 100,000 is the maximum amount that can be awarded to A.

Example of the impact on the allegations supporting a party's claims of the principle of party representation (*forhandlingsmaksimen*): A purchased a house, or a business, from B. Now, it is alleged by A that the house, respectively the business, has defects, and A raises a claim against B for compensation. A supports his claim with the argument that B had not given all relevant information to A during the negotiations before the deal was done, and that therefore, B is liable on the grounds of *culpa* (negligence). However, at the end of the oral hearing, the court did not find this allegation supported by the facts proved during the trial. A could have supported his claim with a subsidiary argument, i.e., that the defect is of such a serious nature that A should be rewarded a price reduction on purely objective grounds, e.g., one-fourth or one-third of the purchase price paid and that such price reduction can be awarded without negligence having been proved. However, A does not support his claim with such a subsidiary allegation.

Consequently, the court cannot take such possible subsidiary allegation (Danish: *subsidiært anbringende*) into consideration, and the court will have to acquit the defendant, although the court clearly sees that such a subsidiary allegation would have had a fair chance of being supported by the court.

18. The main rule in Danish procedure is that court cases are tried orally when the pretrial is finalized ('court cases shall be heard orally') (cf. *Rpl* section 148, subsection 1, 1st sentence). This applies to both civil and criminal cases.

However, some types of cases are tried in writing. The main rule is that appeals against orders and rulings concerning procedural questions ('formality' of the case) are reviewed in writing by the Court of Appeal.

Since the Court Reform 2007/2008, also cases in first instance (*Rpl* section 366), as well as appeals against judgments (*Rpl* section 387), *may* be heard in writing, particularly if the parties can agree to make a joint request to the court to do so, but also in some other cases. The number of cases that are decided in writing is increasing (today between one-third and half of the cases before the Supreme Court), and no doubt it leads to more rational use of the courts' resources. A certain reluctance on the part of the lawyers may very well be traced, perhaps because lawyers are afraid that their clients will not be able to see for themselves how much is being done to win their case. However, as mentioned, the Supreme Court mostly deals with civil cases in writing if the case does not involve questions of fact-finding and if this can speed up the case. A case cannot be tried in writing unless the facts are so clear that there is no need for new evidence to be produced. This is quite often the case in the Supreme Court. Cases which only concern points of law may, therefore, be well suited to written procedure.

19. Court hearings, including the trial, employ free speech (cf. *Rpl* section 148, subsection 2). This includes the parties and witnesses who are being examined, and who may not limit themselves to reading written declarations aloud, but must freely answer the questions directed to them. They may only rely on notes and documents to the extent permitted by the court (cf. *Rpl* section 184, subsection 3), but such permission is of course practically always given.

Witnesses are under an obligation to refresh their knowledge of the case before appearing in court (cf. section 180).

The Court Reform 2007/2008 introduced the concept of written statements from witnesses (cf. *Rpl* section 297), either where the parties agree or where the court permits the use of such statement because the court finds it unproblematic, and such written statements are gradually augmenting in numbers. However, the use of written witness statements does not at all have a proportion under Danish procedural law as we know it under, for example, United States (US) or United Kingdom (UK) procedural law (witness depositions, etc.), or as we know it from International Court of Arbitration (ICC) or London Court of International Arbitration (LCIA) proceedings. Written witness statements will remain an exception under Danish procedural law. Such written statements are primarily suitable for such witnesses who are by no means 'key witnesses' of the case, and where the need for cross-examination does not exist.

Please observe that a written witness statement is not a supplement to oral evidence from the witness, but that the written statement will normally *replace* the oral evidence from that witness. Thus, Danish procedural law has no intention of applying the procedure known from US or UK procedural law, where the written statement (deposition) is only a kind of introduction to the oral evidence from that witness, and where the evidence from the witness is established as a combination of his written and his oral statements.

Only when speaking of surveyors (*skønsmænd*), a different approach is made; they produce a written report to the court and the parties, and very often they are invited to supplement their report through oral evidence before the court (so-called *afhjemling*, certification), where a party may, through his examination of the surveyor, seek to 'undermine' the observations and conclusions of the surveyor.

20. Before the Court Reform 2007/2008, the oral procedure in court was rather stiff and lengthy. As an example, the central parts of the documents would normally be read out in court to allow the parties, the court and the audience to hear all that has a bearing on the case. When, for example, a civil case was heard, counsel for the plaintiff would have to not only present the case to establish a general overview of the nature of the disagreement but also read out the relevant parts of the documents produced.

Considering, however, that the courts of many other countries are eminently capable of observing the principle of open trial, while spending much less time on the trial without injuring the rule of law, a considerable scope existed for contracting court hearings and making them more efficient by cutting out the reading of written materials in whole or in part, under the assumption that they are known in advance – and this is exactly what has been done through the Court Reform 2007/2008.

Consequently, the plaintiff should normally limit himself to presenting the case, and to draw the court's attention to especially important parts of the documents, without necessarily reading *all* such parts aloud. Both the Supreme Court and the two High Courts, the Western and the Eastern High Court, have issued guidelines for lawyers on how to present, through the written extract of the case, which parts of the documents they attach most importance to, so members of the court are well prepared for the oral hearing when concentrating on the writs produced by the parties, and the highlighted parts of the documents of the case.

However, it must be admitted that the old traditions have survived. Although parties can now assume that members of the court have read at least the parts of the documents that have been marked in advance by the parties, *the oral presentation of the case* still spends a considerable portion of time reading aloud large parts of the documents. It would seem that we are in a transition phase, and advocates do not quite trust that they can skip reading large portions of the documents aloud. When doing so, they are often not stopped by the court. So the prudent advocate prepares himself or herself for reading large parts of the case aloud in court, and the prudent judge reads those large parts of the case in advance, and does not stop the advocate who reads those large parts aloud. Add to this that parties and witnesses are, as mentioned, heard before the court, it is clear that the oral hearing in cases takes its time in Denmark; however, you can be sure that the judge, when deciding in your case, knows *all* relevant aspects of the case.

21. A central element in the production of evidence is the examination of witnesses in both civil and criminal proceedings by the parties to a civil case and the accused in a criminal case.

Witnesses are under a compulsion to speak unless exempted or excluded from doing so. The parties to a civil case are under no obligation to speak, but will normally elect to do so, even gladly do so ('parties' hereby also including, for example, the main shareholder of a company which is party to the case). If a party refuses to give evidence, it may count against him in the weighing up of the evidence (cf. *Rpl* section 344, subsection 2), the so-called optional prejudicial effect (optional because the court is free to decide whether to sanction or not), or in Danish as already mentioned: *fakultativ processuel skadevirkning*. Normally, a party will not refuse to give evidence, but may, when questioned about certain aspects of the case, refuse to answer some of the questions, or he will give vague and uncertain answers, and in such cases, the optional prejudicial effect also applies; in practice, perhaps this is the most important aspect of the optional prejudicial effect.

Both witnesses and the parties deciding to give evidence must speak the truth or risk a penalty for misleading the court (cf. section 158 of the Criminal Code).

II. Fundamental Guarantees

22. The Danish Constitution (Denmark: *Grundloven*) contains a number of provisions aimed at guaranteeing the independence of the judicial system. Matters pertaining to the courts can only be regulated by law, not by ministerial proclamations or similar means: cf. section 61 of the Constitution, which also provides that courts with special jurisdiction (*særdomstole*, meaning a court established *after* the case has arisen) cannot be established (whereas courts of enquiry can be established provided they have no competence to judge the case). There is a special Act on courts of enquiry, seeking to balance on one side the need for fact-finding in cases of public interest, and on the other side the protection of the persons involved who must not be forced to give evidence against themselves, cf. Article 6, subsection 2 of the EHRC.

'In the exercise of their vocation', judges 'shall obey only the law' (cf. section 64, subsection 1, of the Constitution). This means that no other authority can direct them on how to judge in any specific case. To further guarantee their independence, they cannot be dismissed or transferred by government decision (cf. section 64, subsection 2 of the Constitution). They can only be dismissed by judgment (given by the Special Court of Indictment and Revision, *Den Særlige Klageret*).

Under the influence of *Montesquieu*, the Constitution's section 3 establishes the fundamental principle of the tripartite division of power: the legislative power is vested in (monarch and) Parliament – the monarch's part of this being a mere formality; the executive power rests with the monarch, i.e., the government; the judicial power lies with the courts.

The Danish Supreme Court has demonstrated that this division of power must be taken seriously by the Parliament. This happened when a bill (*'Tvindloven', or the Tvind Act*), which in effect settled a disagreement between the government and some private independent schools (the *Tvind* schools) on their use of government subsidies, was set aside by the Supreme Court on the grounds that it contravened section 3 of the Constitution.[11] The disagreements on the schools' use of public funds should not have been settled through an Act of Parliament, but through an *administrative* decision which could then be tried before the courts.

A standing point of criticism over many years was the fact that the Danish courts came under a Ministry (the Ministry of Justice) and were consequently dependent on funding, etc., from there. In order to provide even better security for the courts' independence, extensive reforms were introduced in 1999 which transferred the Minister's competence to a special authority, the Court Administration Board (*Domstolsstyrelsen*), discussed in more detail below, paragraph 44, in the discussion on courts and judges. Also, the competence to appoint new judges was transferred from the Minister to yet a new independent authority, the Judge Appointment Board (*Dommerudnævnelsesrådet*), consisting mainly of representatives for members of the courts, as well as representatives for the 'consumers' of court services.

23. The civil rights (freedoms) arising under the EHRC have been attracting increasing attention in Danish procedural law for quite a number of years now, and we have reached a point where every judge and practising lawyer is well aware that the EHRC (and thereby also the ECHR in Strasbourg) is always present in their minds as a correctional factor, when questions arise of deprivation of personal freedom (Article 5), access to court and fair trial (Article 6), prohibition of retroactive criminal law (Article 7), respect for personal and family life, etc. (Article 8), freedom of religion (Article 9), freedom of expression (Article 10), freedom of assembly and association (Article 11, including the right *not* to enter an association), non-discrimination (Article 14), protection of possessions (Protocol 1, Article 1), etc.

---

11. Cf. *UfR* 1999.841 H.

To mention an example, the Danish Supreme Court has refused, in contrast to all lower instances, to bow to the intentions of the legislative powers and expel foreigners in a number of cases where the court found that there was no proportionality between the crime committed by the person under threat of expulsion and the disruption which an expulsion from Denmark would cause to family life after perhaps many years' residence in this country.[12] In respect of the principle of proportionality, the courts must thus take into consideration: (1) the degree of attachment to Denmark; (2) the degree of attachment to the foreigner's home country; (3) the seriousness and character of the crime committed.

24. Many other examples can be mentioned: The High Courts have, in cases of photo-traps alongside the roads, taken Article 6, subsection 2 of the EHRC and its prohibition against self-incrimination into due consideration, where the person on the photo could not be recognized, and the owner of the car was under a duty to reveal who had driven his car at that particular time. If it could have been himself, his duty to reveal was suspended.[13]

Denmark is at the moment and has actually been working on this reform for a very long period of time, reforming its provisions in the *Rpl* about civil claims being dealt with during criminal cases, for example, the victim's claim for compensation. The reform will probably allow such civil claims to be decided by the court, even if the accused is acquitted in the criminal part of the case, i.e., in such cases where the standards of proof in criminal cases are not met with, but where the standard of proof in civil cases are met with.

This will indeed be a rational way of deciding many civil claims; however, as it was demonstrated in some cases against Norway, the judgment in the civil part of the case must never be shaped in such a way that it might cast doubt on the acquittal in the criminal part of the case, cf. *Orr v. Norway.*[14] We must see to it that the new Danish provisions on civil claims during criminal cases are shaped in such a way that Article 6, subsection 2 of the EHRC is respected. The report from the Danish Civil Justice Council, no. 1522/2010, is still considered by the Ministry of Justice, which indicates that the suggestions on this field are not so easily accepted as most other suggestions coming from the Civil Justice Council. Admittedly, it is very difficult to strike a fair balance between the interests of the victim and the interests of the accused.

The impact of the EHRC is also seen in antitrust cases with so-called *dawn raids*, where civil servants from the Commission in Brussels, assisted by local civil servants from the National Antitrust Authority. The EU Regulation behind such dawn raids would not always seem to give full credit to the prohibition against self-incrimination, cf. Article 6, subsection 2 of the EHRC, and we have seen court orders, issued on the evening before such a dawn raid, ordering the company and its

12. Cf., e.g., *UfR* 1999:271 H, *UfR* 1999:275 H, *UfR* 1999:1390 H and *UfR* 1999:1394 H.
13. Cf. *UfR* 2002:2729 V, whereas if it could not have been himself, his duty to reveal was upheld, cf. *UfR* 2003:1029 V.
14. ECHR judgment of 15 May 2008.

employees and managers to produce all evidence in their possession, regardless of the impact on themselves, and thus regardless of the prohibition against self-incrimination.

The Supreme Court, *Højesteret*, in *Trioplast Nyborg A/S* took a firm stand on this[15] as it corrected the order issued by the city court and upheld by the High Court. The Supreme Court emphasized that the employees could not refuse to produce merely factual information, although such items of information might serve as evidence for violation of the antitrust provisions. However, the courts could not order the company and its employees to answer questions if such answers would force the company to confess illegal actions for which the burden of proof rests with the Commission. This thin, but important red line, which the lower courts had refused to draw, was clearly drawn by *Højesteret*, based on Article 6, subsection 2, thereby of course taking inspiration from *Mannesmannröhrenwerke AG.*[16]

Finally, one could mention the delicate question of whether or not to allow the concept of 'anonymous' witnesses in the *Rpl* – by 'anonymous' meaning that the accused does not know the identity of the witness. After years of debate on this question, and taking into consideration that the ECHR allows such witnesses under a number of strict conditions (cf. *Saïdi v. France* – drugs, *Doorson v. Netherlands* – drugs, and *Mechelen v. Netherlands* – killing of policemen), Denmark joined the nations which allow the use of anonymous witness (*Rpl* section 856), but only in serious cases with personal risks for the witness, where 'the anonymity is without importance for the defence of the accused'.

25. Upon the general incorporation of the EHRC into Danish law with effect from 1 July 1992 – which of course means that the EHRC is not only binding on Denmark as a state on the international level but also that *the EHRC is a part of internal Danish law*, quite on level with (other) Acts of Parliament – it was assumed that Danish courts would be reticent in adopting a new independent interpretation of the EHRC. In other words, judges were expected to use the EHRC only as a 'corrective' to Danish law when they were relatively certain of its interpretation. Every indication is, however, that the Danish courts have already distanced themselves from this original attitude, which implies a cautious and restrictive interpretation of the EHRC. Precedents from Strasbourg are not given a restrictive interpretation by Danish courts but rather a most loyal one.

26. After Denmark was found guilty on 8 February 1996 in the haemophilia cases (where France was also found guilty in Strasbourg for slow handling of the case in the courts), the Danish courts are now taking the EHRC requirement regarding a 'reasonable time' – cf. Article 6, subsection 1 – extremely seriously. In long-running criminal cases, reduced sentences may be given, even where the EHRC may not have been specifically breached. Thus, in *Toldpladesagen*,[17] unconditional sentences were suspended, and in *Nordisk Fjer* a processing time of seven and a half years was found not to be unreasonable in so complex a criminal case, but where,

15. In *UfR* 2003:1328 H.
16. The Court of First Instance's (CFI) decision of 20 Feb. 2001, T 111/98.
17. *UfR* 1997:1291 Ø.

in relation to the accused accountants who were 'only' found guilty of gross negligence, the case was found to have lasted too long, and their sentences were reduced considerably to fines fixed in proportion to their daily income, with absolute discharge in one case.[18]

If the national system provides adequate compensation of its own accord, there is no basis for complaining to the Human Rights Court: cf., for example, the court's decision in *Kelling v. Denmark*,[19] where compensation or partial dismissal had been granted in a protracted drugs case.

The Labour Court (*Arbejdsretten*), which is an instance with special powers in questions concerning labour and industrial relations law, has been in the spotlight with regard to the question of impartiality, especially with regard to the former rules for judges appointed by various organizations whose impartiality in relation to the party who had not appointed a judge(s) could in principle be brought into doubt. Important changes were enacted in 1997: Under the former section 1, the ordinary members and deputies of the Labour Court were appointed by the various employer and employee organizations as well as public bodies. Now, ordinary judges and deputy judges are instead appointed for a period of five years by the Minister of Labour following recommendations from the organizations. The aim is to ensure compliance with the right contained in Article 6, subsection 1, of the EHRC concerning impartial judges. The revised rules for the Labour Court are thus a good example of the Danish respect for Article 6.

27. In both civil and criminal cases, the trial ends with the court 'setting down the case for judgment' (i.e., advising the parties that the case now depends on the court's deliberations resulting in a judgment in the case). In 1997, the *Rpl* was tightened in order to ensure speedier handling of civil cases, etc., and these intentions were further followed up through the Court Reform 2007/2008. The reason behind these tighter rules includes the provision contained in Article 6, subsection 1, of the EHRC on a fair trial, which requires proceedings to take place 'within a reasonable time'. The court must now make its decision in civil cases 'with all due speed after the trial has ended', and when the case is set down for judgment or order, the court must indicate when the judgment or order will be given (cf. section 219, subsection 1, 1st sentence, of the *Rpl*). City courts must hand down a judgment or order not later than four weeks after the case has been set down for judgment if the case is heard by a single professional judge. The time limit is two months in city court cases with three judges, and in High Court cases also two months. These limits may, however, be extended in special cases (cf. section 219, subsection 2). In criminal cases, the judgment must be given 'with all due speed after the trial has ended', and the dominant principle is that if judgment cannot be given on the same day, it should follow within a week at the most, in trial by jury not later than the following day (cf. section 219a, subsection 1).

28. Judgments and interlocutory orders, but not opinions, must be reasoned (cf. section 218, subsection 1). The reasoning, or *ratio decidendi*, in Danish called the

18. *UfR* 1998:1752 Ø.
19. Of 2 Feb. 1999.

premises (from Latin: *praemittere* – to send before, i.e., before the concluding words or judgment as such, which is preceded by the words '*THI KENDES FOR RET: ...* ', the word '*THI*' meaning: Therefore, ...) can act both as guidance for the parties and as a source of information for others on what the state of law is in the area considered in the judgment. The grounds for a judgment play an important role, not least when the parties decide whether or not to appeal the decision. The requirement that judgments must be reasoned is also important for the law, as it presumably contributes to guaranteeing the best possible decisions.

If one or more of the deliberating judges disagree with the result or reasoning of the majority, the judgment is given with dissent, by name or anonymously. In all Supreme Court cases, civil and criminal, the dissenting judge's name must be specified. The same applies to all civil High Court cases (whether in first or second instance). Anonymous dissent may occur in criminal cases in city courts and the High Court (but if the dissenting judge is the city court judge who wants to acquit in a case where the lay judges do not, this must appear in the court records, and the dissent will thus not remain anonymous), and in other cases, for example, with expert lay judges in maritime cases, commercial cases, housing cases in city courts, etc. It must be presumed that the dissenting judge has the right to give his dissent in his name in cases where the law merely specifies anonymous dissent.

29. The classical structure of a judgment in a civil case is thus: (1) the essential facts of the case and the points of dispute (*narratio*); (2) summary documentation (relevant parts of the written materials); (3) claims; (4) testimony by the parties; (5) testimony by witnesses; (6) summary of procedure; (7) the reasoning (premises); (8) the judgment (conclusion): '*THI KENDES FOR RET:* ... '. It will be seen that Danish judgment 'work' themselves up to the conclusion, contrary to some other countries where the conclusions are highlighted in the first parts of the judgment.

Earlier, judgment was pronounced in both civil and criminal cases by the judge reading out the final judgment (the conclusion) '*THI KENDES FOR RET:* ... ' in a court sitting. Now, in civil cases, the judgment is uploaded to the digital platform and the parties notified so that they can access it. In criminal cases, the judgment must normally be read aloud in a court meeting.

When applying the word 'sending', it must be noted that judgments are normally not sent to parties and advocates on paper, but rather *delivered in their secured digital mailbox*. For a private citizen, the mailbox is under http://www.borger.dk (= 'citizen.dk'), and for advocates and other businesses, the mailbox is under http://www.virk.dk (= 'business.dk'). Privacy is guaranteed through a sophisticated system applying a combination of: (1) user name; (2) access code; (3) additional personal code possessed on paper by the citizen or business.

This digital system allows an advocate to be in possession of a PDF version of the judgment minutes after it was officially pronounced by the court.

Following a pilot project period during 2017, since 2018, the communication between the courts and the parties and lawyers is fully digitalized and is being handled through the 'digital case portal' of the Danish courts. Access to the relevant cases in the portal is upon registration granted to the parties and their representatives, and surveyors.

30. In 2004, the *Rpl* was reformed in order to improve the public's access to documents concerning trials, both civil and criminal. As a main rule, everyone, without having to prove special interest in the case, has a right to obtain copies of judgments, however with prior anonymization in criminal judgments. There is no general access to all documents in civil or criminal cases, but some important documents are subject to public access. If in a civil case, the parties have summarized their claims and allegations before the oral hearing, such writs (called *sammenfattende processkrift* – summarizing writ, and *påstandsdokument* – summary of claims) are subject to public access. The advocate and his or her client should always have this in mind – that what they write in the summarizing writ is in reality also disclosed to the public (although journalists do not always think about this possibility).

Part I. Judicial Organization

Chapter 1. The Courts and Their Members

§1. Courts

I. Structure of the Court System

31. As specified by section 1 of the *Rpl*, the so-called ordinary courts are the Supreme Court (*Højesteret*, cf. section 2); the Eastern High Court and the Western High Court (*Østre Landsret*, *Vestre Landsret*, cf. sections 5–8); the city courts (*byretterne*, cf. sections 9–13); the Maritime and Commercial Court (*Sø- og Handelsretten*, cf. sections 15–17, and sections 4–5 of the Bankruptcy Act); and the Land Registration Court (*Tinglysningsretten*, cf. section 18).

32. The Supreme Court (*Højesteret*) in Copenhagen comprises the President of the Court and (for the time being) fifteen other judges. The Supreme Court functions solely as a Court of Appeal. Its jurisdictional district is the entire kingdom of Denmark. It sits only in Copenhagen. Very important cases are heard and decided by the full bench. This applies particularly to cases in which the constitutionality of an Act is in question, and it is also customary for the full Court to sit if a candidate for the office of Supreme Court judge is taking part in the deliberations on a trial basis (four times).

33. The Eastern High Court (*Østre Landsret*) sits in Copenhagen and comprises the President of the Court and fifty-six other judges, while the Western High Court (*Vestre Landsret*) sits in Viborg and comprises the President of the Court and thirty-six other judges. The jurisdiction of the Eastern High Court comprises Copenhagen and the Danish islands, while the jurisdiction of the Western High Court includes all Jutland. The High Court functions as Court of First Instance (Luxembourg) (CFI) (civil cases of principal importance, referred to the High Court from a city court) and as Court of Appeal (civil cases and criminal cases appealed from a city court, whether they have been decided by one professional judge and two lay judges, or by three professional judges and six jurors).

When the High Court acts as CFI, which after the Court Reform 2007/2008 as mentioned only will happen in civil cases referred to the High Court because they are of principal importance, its decisions may freely be submitted to the Supreme Court. Since the Court Reform 2007/2008, which has changed the city courts into becoming the Courts of First Instance in both civil and criminal cases, the function of the High Court has changed, making it predominantly a Court of Appeal.

When acting as a Court of Appeal, the High Court's decisions can only be taken to the Supreme Court if leave to appeal to a third instance is granted by the Appeals Permission Board (*Procesbevillingsnævnet*).

34. City courts (*byretter*), of which there are now twenty-four (against eighty-two before the Court Reform 2007/2008), each cover a particular district, and many city courts have several judges, one of the main ideas behind the reform being to reshape the city courts in order to make them larger and allowing the judges to specialize. The largest of the city courts, the Copenhagen City Court, has not less than thirty-eight judges plus the President of the court.

All civil cases are now brought before the city courts as first instance (which can, as mentioned, refer a case with the principal and fundamental issue to the High Court in the first instance). Also, all criminal cases are now brought before the city courts. In criminal cases, there are three options: (1) a smaller criminal case, where no imprisonment is at stake: one professional judge; (2) a more serious case where less than four years imprisonment is at stake: one professional judge and two lay judges; (3) very serious cases where at least four years imprisonment is at stake: three professional judges and six jurors.

35. In civil cases, the case is usually heard by one professional judge, but after the Court Reform 2007/2008, it is possible to have the case heard and decided by three professional judges. Also, it is possible to have a combination of one professional judge plus two co-judges who are specialists in the field, for example, business questions, which the case is concentrated on. A combination of three professional judges and two (and in special cases, four) specialist judges is also possible. During the pretrial phase, the parties have to pronounce their wishes concerning a tribunal consisting of more than one professional judge.

Business undertakings – but not consumers – may in advance (and already in their contract, if they wish to do so) waive their right of appeal after the judgment in the city court, and such a waiver may be under the condition that the case is heard and decided by three professional judges. Through such an arrangement the procedure can come rather close to arbitral proceedings – which is exactly the idea with these provisions in the *Rpl.* The only difference from arbitration is, of course, that the parties at trial before a court cannot themselves elect their judges, contrary to what is possible in arbitral proceedings with an ad hoc tribunal composed by the parties themselves.

36. The city courts are responsible not only for legal proceedings but also for a number of other judicial tasks, as distinct from administrative functions (cf. section 14):

- city courts thus act as probate and bankruptcy courts – under the name: *skifteretten* (which is just a specialized part of the city court) (i.e., with responsibility for the administration mainly of deceased estates and estates in cases involving separation or divorce, estates in liquidation, debt rescheduling, compositions with

creditors, and suspensions of payment). However, please note that cases of bankruptcy and debt rescheduling in the area of Greater Copenhagen are dealt with by The Maritime and Commercial Court (*Sø- og Handelsretten*), *see* paragraph 42 below;
- bailiff's court (i.e., with responsibility for executions, forced sales, injunctions and seizure, as also enforcement proceedings involving other than cash claims such as repossession);
- notary public (i.e., last wills and testaments, protests against bills, drawing of lottery tickets and certification of copies);
- collection of court fees (e.g., in connection with the filing of a writ when an action is brought before the court), including probate fees and taxes on deceased estates, formerly inheritance tax.

Up till 2009 city courts also acted as registrar (i.e., with responsibility for the registration of land titles, mortgage in motor vehicles, chattel mortgages, marriage contracts, etc.), but the Land Registration Court (*Tinglysningsretten*), placed for all Denmark in the city of Hobro, Jutland, has from the autumn of 2009 taken over this highly specialized and digitalized function.

37. Tenancy cases are taken to the housing tribunal in the first instance. The tribunal is – again – the city court, i.e., the city court placed in the district where the property is situated. All disputes concerning industrial and other commercial leasing are heard in the first instance by this tribunal. Decisions made by local rent tribunals (*huslejenævn*) in cases concerning household rent are reviewed by this court if one of the parties wishes to bring the case before the court.

38. The Danish Maritime and Commercial Court (*Sø- og Handelsretten*) is a rather small court, only having five professional judges, including the court's President and its two vice presidents. The court, furthermore, has around one hundred expert judges, appointed by the President of the Court, normally on a proposal from organizations generally recognized by the business community. When hearing cases, the court sits in chambers presided by the court's President or one of its vice presidents or judges, together with two or four expert judges appointed by the Chamber's President for each individual case on the basis of the sort of expertise(s) appropriate to settle that case. Particularly important or difficult cases may be heard by a chamber composed of three professional judges, one of them acting as the Chamber's President, sitting together with two or, eventually, four expert judges.

The court has its seat in Copenhagen, but where appropriate it may decide to sit and hear individual cases in other parts of the country. This possibility was introduced through the Court Reform 2007/2008, which also extended the Maritime and Commercial Court's jurisdiction to the entire country, and at the same time permitted this specialist court to concentrate on cases, in which its expertise is most useful.

39. One of the Maritime and Commercial Court's primary competences is to deal with all 'international cases in which expertise in international business questions is of significant importance' (*Rpl* section 225, subsection 2, no. 1), and in that connection the concept 'International cases' is interpreted broadly, so that *inter alia*, the parties do not necessarily have to be located in different countries.

Also, this court is specialized in Intellectual Property (IP) cases, thus dealing with most of the cases on patents, trademarks, etc., in Denmark, cf. further below, paragraph 42.

Furthermore, cases from city courts can be referred to the Maritime and Commercial Court in principal matters where knowledge of business law is of significant importance.

40. The Maritime and Commercial Court, unlike other Danish courts, accepts evidence, especially the presentation of documents and the hearing of witnesses, in English and German. However, under the Rpl, the court cannot – like an arbitration tribunal – deviate from Danish as the language of the proceedings and permit the parties to make their submissions in other languages than Danish.

41. The Maritime and Commercial Court's judgments could until 1 February 2014 be appealed directly to the Danish Supreme Court without any permission, and foreign business entities normally saw this as a further advantage of having their cases dealt with by the Maritime and Commercial Court instead of another Danish court or arbitration tribunal.

With effect as from 1 February 2014, the possibility of appeal from the Maritime and Commercial Court to the Supreme Court has been somewhat restricted. As a main rule, judgments pronounced by the Maritime and Commercial Court are now appealed to the Appeal Court (Western or Eastern High Court, *Vestre Landsret* or *Østre Landsret*) where the case would have been dealt with if it had not been treated by the Maritime and Commercial Court. However, some cases may be appealed directly to the Supreme Court. The case must be of principal character and must have a general importance for the administration and development of law, or the case must have a considerable impact for society, or 'other special reasons' must be in favour of the direct appeal to the Danish Supreme Court. It is obvious, and also appears from the motives for this Act, that these restrictions are created in order to take some of the workloads from the Supreme Court. 'Other special reasons' may, again according to the motives for the Act, be the international character of the case. The criteria 'other special reasons' was not fulfilled in *Monjasa A/S*, a case concerning international trade with bunker oil.[20] Neither was it fulfilled in *Lionheart Project Logistics Inc.* where the question was whether there was a binding agreement on sea transport from Thailand to Turkey.[21] In both cases, there was 'only' a question of interpretation of the parties' contract, which is obviously not enough to fulfil the criterion 'other special reasons'.

42. The jurisdictional competence of the Danish Maritime and Commercial Court also comprises cases concerning EU and Danish competition law. Claims for compensation for breach of competition law must be brought before this Court. The Maritime and Commercial Court is, *inter alia*, also competent in cases to which the

20. Cf. *UfR* 2014.2865 H.
21. Cf. *UfR* 2015.72 H.

Danish Consumer Ombudsman (*Forbrugerombudsmanden*) is a party, i.e., cases concerning unfair market behaviour by one or more business undertakings.

Finally, it should be mentioned that a special branch of the Maritime and Commercial Court deals with bankruptcy cases, including cases of debt rescheduling (*gældssanering*). The competence of this branch of the court only covers Greater Copenhagen, i.e., the areas which would normally be submitted to the competence of the city courts of Copenhagen, Frederiksberg, Glostrup and Lyngby (all situated around the city of Copenhagen). A peculiar feature is that the bankruptcy branch's decisions may be appealed – not to the Supreme Court but to the Eastern High Court.

43. One highly specialized court is the Special Court of Indictment and Revision, *Den Særlige Klageret*, which normally sits in Copenhagen, although most cases are heard in writing. The court comprises three judges, one Supreme Court judge, one High Court judge and one city court judge. In cases concerning the reopening of a criminal case or the disqualification of a defence lawyer, two additional judges always join the bench, one of which must be a practising lawyer and the other a university professor of law (cf. section 1a, subsection 3 of the *Rpl*).

The court's competence has been extended several times. It presently covers the following areas:

- whether a criminal case, having no further avenue of appeal or revision, should be retried by a court in which it has already been heard, typically because new evidence has emerged (cf. sections 975–987). For example, the so-called *Pedal-Ove* case concerning a well-known musician who was found guilty of having killed his wife, but who was acquitted on retrial. Another example is the case of the Kastrup Airport killings where the accused were acquitted but where they could not help boasting of the killings which they had actually committed and were afterwards accused for the second time, and this time found guilty;
- whether disciplinary measures should be taken against a judge;
- whether a lawyer whom a court has refused to call as defence lawyer (or whose authorization is withdrawn) must nonetheless be called to appear for the accused.

Please observe who joins the bench in this Special Court in some of the types of cases mentioned above: three professional judges (Supreme, High Court and city court), one practising lawyer, one professor of law. This idea has been reused concerning the Appeals Permission Board (*Procesbevillingsnævnet*).

II. Administration of the Courts

44. Until 1999, the courts were administered by the Ministry of Justice. However, with effect from 1999, major changes were introduced into the organization of courts. A special administration body – the Danish Court Administration (*Domstolsstyrelsen*) – was established. The Administration is an independent and impartial government institution with responsibility for matters pertaining to court administration and financing: operations, budgets, staff, buildings, technology, etc.

III. Bench and Ministère Public

45. Denmark applies no advocate generals, as they are known from EU justice and some countries. The courts thus receive no 'help' in this way. However, in each case where the state or a state institution is involved, the public is represented by the Attorney to the Treasury (*Kammeradvokaten*), and the arguments of the Attorney to the Treasury often weigh very heavily in the minds of the judges.

IV. Appointment of Judges

A. *General Introduction*

46. As mentioned above, paragraph 44, until 1999, the courts belonged to the Ministry of Justice, and it was this Ministry which in effect 'appointed' the judges. Appointments were made by recommendation from the courts (the presidents of the courts), and the Ministry followed recommendations almost without exception. From this year, the competence to make recommendations to the Minister passed to a special council for the appointment of judges – the Judicial Appointments Council (*Dommerudnævnelsesrådet*) – which makes recommendations to the Ministry of Justice. The Council consists mainly of representatives for members of the courts, as well as representatives for the 'consumers' of court services. The formal requirements for being appointed as judge would not seem to be so difficult to overcome, but in practice the candidate is normally not appointed unless he or she has been through one or more terms in one of the two appeal courts; thereby being closely 'observed' by the judges and thereby having been given a considerable workload, including participating in court, writing the first draft for judgments, etc.

B. *End of Functions*

47. Judges, as well as other civil servants employed at the courts, are automatically dismissed with effect from the end of the month in which they complete their seventieth year (section 34, subsection 2, of the Danish Civil Servants Act, *tjenestemandsloven*). However, if the geographical districts of Danish courts are changed, dismissal may take place of the judges concerned when they have completed their sixty-fifth year (Article 64 of the Danish Constitution, *grundloven*). A judge who has completed his or her sixty-fifth year may agree with the relevant court president to work on part-time if this is compatible with the organization of that specific court (*Rpl* section 51a). A judge who is dismissed for any of these reasons finalizes and decides such cases that he or she has commenced as a judge. This also goes for judges who are not permanent but deputy judges.

C. Incompatibilities and Discipline

48. The *Rpl* contains a number of important provisions which all serve the purpose of securing that the individual judge is, and also appears to be, independent of any kind of special interest and that the judge behaves properly in his or her contact with anyone appearing in court. The options of a judge to hold any kind of sideline are very limited. A permanent sideline is only acceptable if the law prescribes that such a post must be held by a judge, e.g., certain appeal boards of public interest, or if the Judge Appointment Board (*Dommerudnævnelsesrådet*) allows it in each individual case (*Rpl* section 47a, subsection 1). An ad hoc sideline, such as acting as the chairman of an arbitration tribunal, must be accepted in each case by the relevant court president (*Rpl* section 47a, subsection 3). However, judges being authors of scholarly books and articles do not require any acceptance for this. The individual judge's income from sidelines must not, measured for three-year periods, exceed 50% of the judge's ordinary salary as a judge, again with the exception for *inter alia* income from scholarly books and articles (*Rpl* section 47b, subsection 1). Each year before 1 February, each judge must disclose the number and nature of the sidelines for the past year, as well as the income achieved from each sideline (*Rpl* section 47c).

49. During main oral hearings, any judge has to wear a gown (*Rpl* section 56a), blue in city courts, crimson red in the Supreme Court, and black in other courts, including the two appeal courts; the idea of prescribing gowns as mandatory is to 'neutralize' the appearance of the personality of the individual judge. Judges are also forbidden to act in any way in court that could appear as a statement of the judge's religious or political affiliation (*Rpl* section 56).

50. Anyone who finds himself offended by a judge's way of acting towards him or her can file a complaint over the judge to the Special Court of Indictment and Revision, *Den Særlige Klageret* (*Rpl* section 49).

§2. Members of the Judiciary

51. Judges are high-ranking civil servants appointed by royal decree, and their independence of government and Parliament with regard to deciding any individual case is guaranteed by the Constitution (cf. section 64, 1st sentence of the Constitution): 'In the exercise of their vocation, judges shall obey only the Law.' Reference may also be made to the requirement regarding independence and impartiality in Article 6 of the EHRC. The phrase 'by royal decree' means that the appointment is signed by the Danish Queen and a minister of the Crown (cf. section 14, 3rd sentence, of the Constitution). The government cannot dismiss a judge before pensionable age as judges can only be dismissed by judgment (cf. section 64, 2nd sentence, of the Constitution) pronounced by the Special Appeal Court (*Rpl* section 49). Judges are titled Supreme Court judge (*højesteretsdommer*), High Court judge (*landsdommer*) and judge (*dommer*) (*Rpl* section 42).

52. A judge may be partial and must of course then be disqualified for the case. If the judge has his work in a court with several judges, another is appointed in his place, but in courts with only a single judge, a deputy judge from another jurisdiction must be appointed by the President of the High Court.

A case of specific disqualification exists if:

- the judge is a party to the case, has an interest in its outcome or was injured in the crime to be tried;
- the judge is related to one of the parties;
- the judge is related to a lawyer, a prosecutor, etc. (it is the judge who must 'withdraw', not the lawyer);
- the judge has acted in the same case as lawyer, prosecutor or judge in a lower court, etc.;
- in a criminal case, the judge has previously been close to deciding on the question of guilt, for example, by issuing a warrant for the arrest of the accused under the special rules on preventive detention in cases of highly probable cause, or by ruling to authorize certain investigative measures which also require strong grounds;[22] or
- other circumstances exist which could engender doubt as to the judge's absolute impartiality, whereby the well-known double test is applied that justice not only must be done but also that justice must be *seen* to be done.

Practical difficulties have been experienced in the interpretation of section 61. Thus, a judge disqualified himself by stating to the defending lawyer on the telephone from the prosecutor's office that his client could be arrested,[23] and a city court judge was disqualified because he made the following comment in the court records when giving a ruling on temporary custody of children: 'As the most likely outcome of the case is that the respondent will be given custody of all three children, the Court finds no reason to grant a stay of proceedings pending the review of a ruling.'[24]

53. As will be clear from the above, the disqualification rules contained in the *Rpl* must always be read in light of the EHRC's Article 6, requiring independence and impartiality of judges. The Court of Human Rights' case law is thus important for understanding the Danish rules of disqualification. The judge must not only *be* impartial (the subjective criterion) he must also be *seen* to be impartial (the objective criterion): justice must not only *be* done but it must also be *seen* to be done. In the impeachment of former Minister of Justice Erik Ninn-Hansen, the defence claimed that the trial judges appointed by the Parliament were not impartial because

22. *See* the judgment of 24 May 1989 by the Human Rights Court in Hauschildt discussed above, para. 12, which gave cause to tighten the Danish provisions, and *UfR* 1990:13 H (Jydebrødrene).
23. *UfR* 1990:634 H.
24. *UfR* 1994:385 Ø.

the Parliament was also the prosecution in the case, but the judges found themselves to be impartial.[25] A later submission from Ninn-Hansen to the Human Rights Court was rejected.

54. It may happen, even in the Supreme Court, that neither the court nor any of the parties are aware that a problem exists. In a case before the Supreme Court, one of the parties told his lawyer after the trial that one of the Supreme Court judges appeared familiar to him from an earlier stage in the case (a tax case). It was found that the judge in question had taken part in deciding the case when serving as an assessor on the National Tax Tribunal but had forgotten all about it. The Supreme Court, on its own initiative, when having been informed by the party's advocate, immediately reassumed the case, of course with other judges, and heard and decided the case again.[26]

55. A judgment given by a partial judge or by a panel of judges of which one was partial can normally be set aside by appealing the case. E.g., the Supreme Court set aside a High Court judgment where one of the High Court judges sitting on a murder trial by jury had previously contributed to the dismissal of an appeal on detention under the special rule of section 762, subsection 2 (highly probable grounds). This rendered the judge partial under section 60, subsection 2. The case was, therefore, remitted for renewed hearing in the High Court.[27] In contrast, a judge who has placed an accused in remand prison is not normally considered partial in relation to a subsequent compensation case.[28]

56. Judges are aided considerably in their work by deputy judges and senior deputy judges. It would be difficult for the bailiff's courts, the probate and bankruptcy courts and the notary's office to function without the use of deputy and senior deputy judges. Senior deputies may also be appointed as a temporary judge with the competence to decide both civil and criminal cases alone in the city court or with a panel of judges in the High Court. Senior deputy judges can to some extent hear evidence in the Supreme Court in the presence of lawyers having authority (*Rpl* section 4).

57. In light of the Constitution's independence requirement in section 64 and the EHRC's impartiality requirement in Article 6, it has been a cause of concern for some years that senior deputy judges who may be dismissed and transferred were able to decide court cases. Thus, the Supreme Court[29] decided that the question regarding the use of temporary judges ought to be decided by legislation.[30] The long-awaited clarification has since been obtained, as both deputy and senior deputy judges have come under the auspices of the Court Administration Board since its institution on 1 July 1999. They are thus removed from the state administration's

25. *See UfR* 1994:409 R, also assessed in light of Art. 6 of the EHRC.
26. *See TfS* 1995:521 H, which cancels *TfS* 1995:359 H.
27. Cf. *UfR* 1992:300 H.
28. Cf. *UfR* 1992:11 V.
29. In *UfR* 1994:536 H.
30. Cf. *UfR* 1995:428 H.

competence (the Ministry of Justice), and the question of dismissal and transfer has been moved to the Court of Last Resort as for the permanent judges. The independence of judges should thus be secured under both the Danish Constitution and the EHRC, and it should be no cause for concern in the future that court cases are heard and decided by temporary judges.

58. Each court has an administration and registry, headed by a clerk of the court or a registrar. The registrar's responsibilities include calculating and billing court costs for cases received, having copies of court records and written materials made, and dealing with a range of administrative issues, etc. The registry is also responsible for dealing with small claims cases, a cheaper small claims procedure, with a more active part to play for the court than in other civil proceedings, being introduced through the Court Reform 2007/2008 for demands up to DKK 50,000, corresponding to approximately EUR 6,700.

59. The small claims procedure cannot be applied if the case concerns questions of considerably complicated factual and/or legal character, but a case of payment of DKK 40,000 for – and possible faults at – a new kitchen floor could hardly be said to be complicated of nature, cf. *Skovby Gulve ApS.*[31] *See also Karin Hilmer*: The case concerned rent of a mooring for a boat at a private quay, and the owner of the boat contested that a lease agreement had been entered into. In both cases, the High Court decided that the case was to be handled under the small claims procedure.[32] The parties may, after a specific litigation has arisen, agree that the case be not comprised by the small claims procedure, but failing such an agreement, the case will be dealt with according to the small claims procedure.[33] The small claims procedure is also applicable in rent cases,[34] recalling that the city court also has the capacity as rent court.

After the reform, the administration of individual city courts also plays a major role in case preparation, advice to the public, pretrial sittings, writing of judgments, etc.

31. Cf. *UfR* 2009:1274 V.
32. *UfR* 2009:1290 V.
33. Cf. *UfR* 2009:1302 V.
34. Cf. *UfR* 2010:330 Ø.

Chapter 2. The Bar

§1. The Exercise of the Legal Profession

I. Conditions for Admission

60. *Advokater*, the common term for solicitors and barristers in Danish, is called to the Bar by the Ministry of Justice (*Rpl* section 119). Apart from the basic requirements such as a law degree, legal competence, etc., candidates must also have three years' practical legal experience, which most acquire in a position as articled clerk to a practising lawyer. Articled clerks undertake a theoretical course which is now obligatory.

II. Rights and Duties

61. The designation *Advokat* is a protected title which nobody else may use (cf. section 120). The title may not be held by lawyers serving as judges or holding other civil service positions (cf. section 122) unless an exception is made by the Minister of Justice. Those who accept such positions must therefore normally deposit their *Advokat* certificates. Of course, advocates from other EU/EEA (European Economic Area) countries are allowed to practise in Denmark in accordance with Directives 77/249 and 98/5.

62. Lawyers may operate their business in private or public companies (cf. sections 124 and 127a). In the case of legal proceedings, it is not the company, however, but the individual lawyer who represents the client in court.[35] If a lawyer incurs liability for damages to a client, both the company and the lawyer are liable for the claim. All lawyers must take out professional indemnity insurance to cover wrongful acts and omissions. Only lawyers and other legal firms may be shareholders in a law company. However, less than 10% of capital and votes in the company may be owned by non-advocates, for example, employees of the company; the word 'share partner' is seen applied for this but not authorized by the *Rpl.* Apart from this, company law rules apply to the company, for example, with regard to required capital and the preparation of annual accounts.

63. It is normally the lawyer's own decision whether he wants to accept a case or not (cf. section 125), but if the lawyer has applied for and has been appointed to represent parties on legal aid (normally advertised within the jurisdiction), he must also provide legal assistance to persons fulfilling the requisite financial conditions (cf. section 128, subsection 1).

64. In questions of seeking advice, it is of course optional whether one seeks the counsel of a lawyer, an accountant, a consultant or similar, or manages on one's

35. *See UfR* 1992:672 V by implication.

own. The same applies when asked to appear before an administrative authority, for example, the tax department, with an adviser; before such administrative organs, the lawyers hold no kind of sole competence. When it comes to an appearance in court, however, lawyers hold sole competence, generally speaking, to conduct court cases for others (cf. sections 131 and 260), i.e., to act as representative for another person in court. However, a number of exceptions allow for non-advocates to represent a party before a court. The most important exceptions are that a party can be represented by a member of his family and that business undertakings can be represented by one of their employees, provided that this employee has been employed by the company for at least one month, and that he or she has not been hired with the sole purpose of representing the company in court.

65. There is no obligation in civil cases to appear with or be represented by a lawyer (*Rpl* section 259, subsection 1) on presenting a case in person. However, the court may recommend to a party that the assistance of a lawyer be obtained, and it may order the party to do so if the case cannot otherwise be heard in a proper manner. If such order is not followed, the party in question will be deemed to have failed to appear unless the court decides instead to assign counsel (cf. section 259, subsection 3).

Unless the accused in a criminal case has his own defence lawyer (a so-called appointed counsel), a counsel is assigned to the defendant in the more serious types of cases.

66. The Attorney to the Treasury (*Kammeradvokaten*) is a practising lawyer enjoying a special status, which may not be confused with *Rigsadvokaten*, the Director of Public Prosecutions, or a *statsadvokat*, District Attorney. While the latter two distinctly represent the Crown, *Kammeradvokaten* is a private lawyer with whom the government, represented by the Ministry of Finance, has entered into a contract under which he or she provides assistance to the government in a wide range of case types where the state's economic interests are at stake. In cases where a case is brought against the state in a civil matter, the state will always be represented by the Attorney to the Treasury. Where public authorities have doubt whether they should accept responsibility for their behaviour or mistakes and whether they should offer compensation to the other party, a legal opinion from the Attorney to the Treasury will often be decisive for the outcome of the case; if *Kammeradvokaten* recommends the public authority to accept its responsibility, this will often be the outcome of the case. During the years 2017–2018, a certain degree of outsourcing has taken place, thereby reducing the 'monopoly' of the *Kammeradvokaten.* A number of legal fields have been entrusted to other skilled law firms, and at the same time, the *Kammeradvokaten* has been allowed to take new clients in within legal fields where the 'monopoly' of the *Kammeradvokaten* has been broken.

III. Discipline

67. Advocates must act in a way that is consistent with good professional conduct, *god advokatskik* (*Rpl* section 126, subsection 1). The advocate must also execute his assignments with care and scrupulosity, and with due regard to the legitimate interests of the clients. The advocate must not demand a higher fee than what must be considered as fair (*Rpl* section 126, subsection 2).

68. A person or a company that wishes to complain over an advocate, either about the advocate's behaviour or about his or her fee in a specific case, can bring this matter before the Disciplinary Board of the Danish Bar and Law Society (*Advokatnævnet*) in Copenhagen. Disputes on lawyer's fees can also be taken to court, and the same, of course, goes for questions concerning an advocate's tort liability.

§2. Public Institutions and Private Organizations

69. Before 2008, all advocates had to be members of the Danish Bar and Law Society, but after Denmark was found in breach of EHRC Article 11 by the ECHR in a case of negative freedom of association, i.e., the right *not* to be a member of an association,[36] the *Rpl* was reformed in 2008. Today, the Bar and Law Society has only disciplinary competence towards advocates and also plays an important role in commenting on bills of Parliament concerning fundamental questions, but each lawyer must decide for himself whether or not he wants to be a member of an association for lawyers. Actually, a new association (*Danske Advokater*, The Association of Danish Law Firms) has been established, playing an important role in questions like seminars, publications, education, etc., for advocates. Each practising advocate must take education for fifty-four hours every three years, thereby securing that advocates are at any time up-to-date.

70. The Ministry of Justice appoints a number of lawyers in each jurisdiction, on whom the court may call to represent parties with free legal aid who do not express a wish to be represented by a particular lawyer (cf. section 333 of the *Rpl*).

Court-assigned counsels must also provide free legal assistance to people approaching them with a legal problem who fulfil the financial conditions for obtaining legal aid (for which the lawyer must see evidence).

The point is that much legal advice is given in cases where no proceedings are brought, and the lawyer's advice may precisely be that no action should be taken because the client is likely to lose the case. Lawyers not associated with the scheme may apply to join if they so desire.

36. Cf. *Sørensen and Rasmussen v. Denmark*, judgment of 11 Jan. 2006.

Chapter 3. The Bailiffs

§1. Bailiffs

71. The bailiff's court (Danish: *fogedretten*) is a part of the local city court. The bailiff's court is often manned by younger judges who are on the way upwards in their carrier. However, it must be borne in mind that these young assistant judges (Danish: *dommerfuldmægtig* or concerning the more mature of them: *retsassessor*) very often have their theory from the university in fresh memory. They are often bolder and theoretically well educated than older judges.

The bailiff's court has various important competences. The Danish legal philosopher professor, dr.jur. & phil. *Alf Ross* ('On Law and Justice', Danish: 'Om ret og retfærdighed') defined the concept of 'valid law' as a set of rules on the application of physical force, applied by a competent public authority. If we accept this definition of law, we are here, with the introduction of the bailiff's court, in the phase where physical force, if necessary, is applied to enforce the legal provisions.

The bailiff's tasks are:

(1) The bailiff enforces judgments, as well as debt instruments that declare themselves immediately enforceable.
(2) Even without judgment in your hands, you can turn directly to the bailiff and have your claim enforced, provided that your claim does not exceed DKK 100,000 (app. EUR 13,400), and also provided that the alleged debtor has no objections against your claim. If he or she has objections, the bailiff must dismiss the claim and refer it to be treated by the ordinary court.
(3) It is the bailiff that administers forced sale of real estate and other kinds of property.
(4) The bailiff takes care of enforcing claims that are not of an economic character but rather focused on persons or things. Thus, the bailiff can help with enforcing:
   (a) a parent's visitation rights after a divorce;
   (b) a lessor's right to be reinstalled in the possession of leased goods after the termination of the leasing contract;
   (c) more generally, a person's right to get back things that have been leased or lent to another person.

One competence the bailiff had until 1 July 2013 but which has now been transferred to other instances (*see* immediately below) is the competence in *injunction* cases. If a person wishes to stop another company from violating his or her IP rights (patents, trademarks, copyrights, etc.), he or she would under Danish procedural law, before 1 July 2013, turn to the bailiff, and ask him or her to forbid the use of the patent, trademark, or copyright. From 1 July 2013, one must turn to the court that is competent to treat the subject matter of the case, and this court will act in the same way (however, perhaps with even greater skills) as the bailiff before 1 July 2013.

More about this important and practical matter below, paragraph 173, when discussing injunction.

§2. AUTHORIZED DEBT COLLECTION BUSINESS

72. A special Act on debt collection was introduced in Denmark with effect from 1997 (*inkassoloven*). The Act does not apply to debt collection by public authorities (cf. section 1, subsection 3). Basically, the Act applies only to debt collection on behalf of others, i.e., not when a company collects its own debts, but it may have a knock-on effect on this, for instance, with regard to the provision (*see* below, paragraph 73) that sound debt collecting practices must be observed.

A number of the Act's most central provisions also apply to debt collection carried out by lawyers (cf. section 1, subsection 2). This applies, for example, to the central provisions in section 9 on sound debt collecting practices, section 10 on the issuing of reminders before steps are taken to collect the debt, section 12 on making a personal approach to the debtor, section 13 on voluntary return of chattels and section 29 on penalties.

Lawyers are automatically entitled to engage in debt collecting, but everybody else requires special authorization (cf. section 3 of the Act). Authorization can be given to both natural persons (cf. section 5) and to 'private and public companies registered with the Danish Commerce Agency' (*Erhvervsstyrelsen*) (cf. section 6). Branches of foreign companies are eligible for authorization if 'entitled to authorization by international agreement or as directed by the Minister of Justice' (cf. section 6, subsection 1, last sentence). An authorization is valid for a maximum of five years at a time (cf. section 7). Employees who approach debtors in person must be approved for this (cf. section 8).

73. Debt collection must be performed in accordance with sound debt collection practices (cf. section 9). The provision adds that it is contrary to sound practice to use 'methods which subject a person to unreasonable pressure, injury or nuisance'.

There is an important provision in section 10 to the effect that before subjecting the debtor to 'other measures aimed at collecting a debt', a reminder must be sent by letter, clearly stating all the information required for the debtor's assessment of the claim and allowing a period for payment of not less than ten days from the date on which the letter was sent. Steps to collect the debt may, however, be initiated to the extent that compliance with section 10 would incur 'an obvious risk that the debt may not otherwise be able to be collected' (cf. section 11).

Failure to observe the obligation to issue a reminder will normally have the effect that the plaintiff must pay all court costs.[37]

74. Bankruptcy petitions must also be deemed to be governed by the Debt Collection Act.[38] However, failure to comply with section 10 does not mean that the petition must be rejected. If compliance with section 10 is not clear from the petition, the court must, pursuant to section 8 of the Bankruptcy Act, set a deadline

37. Cf. *UfR* 1999:530 Ø.
38. *See UfR* 1998:1518 H.

within which the applicant must procure the information to prove that the conditions under section 10 or 11 of the Debt Collection Act have been fulfilled before the court decides whether the application should be rejected.[39]

75. Collected money must be kept separate from the debt collection agency's own funds (cf. section 14). It must immediately be deposited in a separate account in a bank unless otherwise agreed with the creditor (cf. section 15), and it must be paid out to the creditor without undue delay unless otherwise agreed. Interest on the amount deposited in principle accrues to the creditor (cf. section 15, subsection 2; *see* section 20, subsection 2).

76. The debt collection agency may not advertise in a manner which may be taken to indicate that it is a kind of legal consultant, legal office or similar (cf. also section 17). The Agency and its employees have a duty of secrecy (cf. section 18). There are special provisions on the withdrawal and lapse of authorizations in sections 21–27. The police have a duty to inspect debt collection agencies and may enter their premises without a court order (cf. section 28). Breach of the Act's central provisions is punishable by fine or lenient imprisonment (cf. also section 29).

39. Jens Paulsen comments in *FM* 1999:18 et seq. that this makes the state of law 'acceptable for the practicing lawyer'.

Part II. Jurisdiction

Chapter 1. Domestic Jurisdiction

§1. Subject Matter Jurisdiction

77. Until 1989, the *Rpl*'s main formal rule on expertise was that civil cases were High Court cases in the first instance. An important exception applied to cases involving money below a certain amount (the 'High Court limit'). In order to relieve the High Courts and send as many cases as possible to the city courts as the first instance, the limit was raised several times. In 1989, resolute action was taken with regard to the de facto trend of several years, and the *Rpl*'s main rule became that civil cases should be heard by city courts as the first instance (cf. section 224). With the Court Reform 2007/2008, the step was taken in full, removing all exceptions to this main rule but one – i.e., the exception that cases raising principal issues can be referred from the city court to the High Court as the first instance.

Case law since the reform has shown that High Courts regard very few cases as 'principal', so the result is that almost any civil case (and all criminal cases) must start in the city court as the first instance. The possibility of referring a case of the first instance to High Court must be regarded in connection with the possibility, also introduced through the Court Reform 2007/2008, of letting three professional judges hear the case (*Rpl* section 12). This is possible not only *if* the case raises principal legal questions but also *if* the outcome of the case might have a considerable impact on others than the parties, *if* the case contains extensive or difficult factual or legal questions, or *if* the special character of the case as an exception makes it suitable with a three or five-judge bench. In *Skodsborg Grundejerforening*, an association of house-owners had sued the state because they had objections, based on the EU Directive on the assessment of the effects of certain public and private projects on the environment, against some public installations near to the coast.[40] Before referring the case to the High Court, the city court must take its own stand on the question of whether the case is principal or not.[41] From case law, it can be seen that it was not enough to regard the case as principal that the issues at stake

40. *UfR* 2007:2922 Ø.
41. Cf. *UfR* 2008:826 V. In *UfR* 2014:342 V, the Western High Court stated that for the case to be referred from the city court to the High Court, it is not enough for the city court to state that it 'cannot exclude' that the case is principal; the city court must assess this question on its own, and can only refer the case to the High Court if the city court positively holds that the case is of principal importance.

concerned the interaction between private insurance and public pension, etc.[42] that some questions of defining the time for the selling of a portion of shares were not regarded as principal, but where the question of Inland Revenue Service's possibility of disagreeing with the figures indicated by the taxpayer after the ordinary time limits for such disagreement was regarded as principal,[43] that legal questions on the interpretation of the special tax provisions allowing house-owners to sell their house, flat, etc., without taxation of the profit as principal.[44]

Since 2014, the High Court can simply send the case back to the city court if the High Court does *not* hold that the case is of principal importance.

The whole idea of this system is to ensure that only cases of principal importance come up to the Danish Supreme Court. They can do so in two ways: (1) either by the High Court accepting the case as a principal case, thus giving way to direct appeal of the merits in the case to the Supreme Court; or (2) by letting the case be treated by the city court and the High Court, and then letting the case be referred to the Supreme Court as the third instance if this is allowed by the Appeals Permission Board (Danish: *Procesbevillingsnævnet).*

§2. Venue (Territorial Jurisdiction)

78. The main rule is that a case must be taken to the defendant's home court (*Rpl* section 235), the element of contact with the court being defined as the defendant's domicile or equivalent. If the defendant has no domicile but is staying in Denmark, the home court is the place where he resides. It is hardly a requirement that the defendant has resided there for any length of time. If the defendant does not even have a place where he resides, the home court is either his last known domicile or place of residence (equal rank). If the defendant moves, the important point is where he lived (or stayed) at the time when the case was brought, i.e., when the writ was submitted to the court (cf. section 348, subsection 1). If the defendant moves after the case has been brought, it may continue in the same court, but it may take a long time before the writ is served if the defendant is difficult to find.

The home court for a legal person or similar (not just legal persons proper such as private or public companies, a foundation or association, but also general and limited partnerships, which are hardly legal persons in the sense of Danish company law) is its main office (cf. section 238). The decisive point for companies is thus not the registered statutory seat, but the de facto main office. On this point, procedural law departs from Danish company law, which is broadly focused on the statutory seat. Procedural law defines the main office as the place where company management is situated.

If it is impossible to find where the company has its de facto main seat, the home court is where merely one member of the board or management is domiciled, a rule which can lead to the existence of several home courts. A company's home court

42. *UfR* 2007:2924 Ø.
43. *TfS* 2008:1089 Ø.
44. *TfS* 2008:1129 H.

can also be used for company-related disputes among company participants themselves, or between the company and its participants, for example, on the reading of statutory pre-emption rights and for disputes between the company or its estate and members of board or management concerning the latter's liability for damages.

79. Exceptional jurisdictions are defined by an element of contact other than domicile or similar. Plaintiff will often prefer to bring an action as close to himself as possible, so the possibility of using an exceptional jurisdiction is often a point of interest. Nevertheless, given Denmark's small size, the question of whether a domestic exceptional jurisdiction can be used does not have quite the same practical importance for the parties as it would if the case involved parties in different countries. The question of whether a plaintiff can use one of the exceptional jurisdictions established by the Brussels I Regulation (which Denmark is part of via parallel convention), which will often lead to a court in the plaintiff's own country, rather than having to go to the defendant's home court, has considerable practical interest.

If a defendant is a natural person running a commercial business, a case involving his business can be taken to the court from where the business is operated, i.e., to the home court for the business (*Rpl* section 237). It is a condition that the business be operated from a given place.

If a company, an association, a general partnership, a trust, etc., conducts business outside the jurisdiction of the company's home court, the case can be instigated where the business is operated, i.e., in the home court of the branch (cf. section 238, subsection 2). The home court of the branch has major significance in cases where, for example, local people trade with the branch of a bank, an insurance company, etc., e.g., in Zürich Forsikring, an insurance company domiciled in Copenhagen could be taken to court in Randers (Jutland), where the company had a branch, in a case concerning the branch.[45] In cases involving agreements, etc., with a branch, clients of, for example, a bank or an insurance company with home court in Copenhagen can thus sue their opponent in the jurisdiction where the branch is located.

A case concerning contract law can be taken to court in the jurisdiction where the obligation from which the case arises was performed or, more importantly, must be performed, i.e., the court of performance (cf. section 242, subsection 1). The court of performance can be used, for example, if suing a building contractor for breach of contract (normally, however, the parties to such contracts would have agreed on arbitration in the Court of Arbitration for Building and Construction Work cf. section 69 of the *AB 18, General Conditions for Work and Supplies*).

The court of performance can also be used, even if the performance of the contract does not require the debtor or his people to be present. As a general rule in Danish law, the court of performance cannot be used in cases involving purely financial claims, such as instruments of debt, overdraft facilities, etc. (cf. section 242, subsection 2); this is, however, entirely different when turning to the Brussels I Regulation, cf. below, paragraph 92, where it is possible to instigate proceedings

45. *UfR* 1992:645 V.

at the place where also a purely financial claims should have been fulfilled, thus in some cases allowing the creditor to instigate proceedings against his debtor at the court of the creditor's own domicile.

Cases involving claims for penalty, damages or redress for breach outside contract can be taken to the court where the wrong was done: cf. section 243 on the court of tort (also called the court of breach or the court of the place of damage). The court of tort is mainly important for cases involving claims for damages outside the contract. In a compensation case, the harmful event can normally be said to have occurred both where the wrong was done and where the damage occurred. The choice between these two locations falls to the plaintiff.

80. It is also worth noting that if plaintiff instigates proceedings in the wrong court within the national boundaries, the case will not be rejected but merely referred to the correct court (cf. section 248, subsection 2, of the *Rpl*), whereas if the proceedings are instigated in a country where the courts do not find themselves competent, the case is dismissed, without being referred to the courts of another country (which is not possible). Danish Courts cannot refer a case to a court on the Faroe Islands.[46]

Apart from the bother and additional costs, the plaintiff's legal rights will not, if the case is referred instead of being rejected, be injured through statute-barring or similar.

81. Those agreements in which two parties may enter into as a forum for the settling of existing or potential disputes fall into the following categories:

(1) *Arbitration agreements:* The parties remove all competence from the courts (in any country) by agreeing to have any dispute settled through arbitration. Arbitration is discussed below in Part X.
(2) *Agreements conferring jurisdiction:* The parties can agree that the dispute should be heard in the first instance (but not in the second instance) by a particular court (cf. section 245, subsection 1). They may, for example, agree that the Western High Court will have jurisdiction if the case would otherwise fall under the Eastern High Court. Or they may agree to confer jurisdiction on the court in city A if the case would otherwise have fallen under another city court, or if the rules on home court and exceptional jurisdiction would otherwise have given plaintiff the choice of several city courts. Parties can only agree on the Maritime and Commercial Court as a venue, if the case by its nature belongs under this court, typically because the case concerns international cases where knowledge of international business matters is of considerable importance (*Rpl* section 225 §2 no. 1).
(3) *One instance:* Business undertakings, but not private persons, can agree that their dispute will only be treated in one instance, thus waiving their possibility of appeal. They can agree on this not only when the dispute has arisen but also in advance (which is new after the Court Reform 2007/2008). Such agreement may be conditional, for example, on the condition that the court accepts the

46. Cf. *UfR* 2009:843 V.

case as a three-judge case (thereby, as already mentioned, obtaining some of the features of arbitral proceedings, however at a lower cost).

In cases concerning consumer agreements, a prior agreement conferring jurisdiction is not binding on the consumer: cf. section 245, subsection 2, of the *Rpl* which was also found to apply to the non-commercial acquisition of a new leisure home, as movable property had been purchased under the same agreement, cf., e.g., *Svend og Kaja Olsen*.[47] It follows *per contra* that jurisdiction agreements entered into both before and after the fact are binding on the business owner, and that jurisdiction agreements entered into after the fact are also binding on the consumer.

An agreement conferring jurisdiction can be entered into tacitly. The most important point to note here is that a tacit agreement will be presumed to have been entered into if the defendant, including consumer defendants, appear in court (or submit a defence in the case of a court where the pretrial stage is conducted in writing with no oral hearings) without objecting to the court's jurisdiction (cf. section 248, subsection 1, 2nd sentence). If, however, the defendant does not attend at all, the court must initiate a check to see if the case has been brought to the right court.

§3. Resolution of Jurisdiction Conflicts

82. The court where the case is launched must carry out a check to see if it is competent to hear the case, given the existing competence distribution among city and High Courts and the special courts (cf. section 232, subsection 1). The court must also check on its own accord that the case is brought to the right court (cf. section 248, subsection 1), however with the exception mentioned just above: that if the defendant does not raise any objection against the venue, this is regarded as a waiver of such objection.

If the case was taken to the wrong court, this court must refer the case to the right court (cf. section 248, subsection 2). Referral is, however, conditional upon another Danish court being competent. A case cannot be referred to a foreign court or arbitration (if the parties have agreed on arbitration, the case must be rejected by the courts if a claim to this effect is made). Another condition of referral is that the court must be able to see, from the case, which is the competent court (cf. the wording of the Act 'the court shall refer the case if possible').

A case is rejected if the court cannot hear it, or if the court has no authority to, or possibility of, referring the case to another Danish court. A case will be rejected if it is found that no Danish court has jurisdiction to hear it, and there is no specific basis for merely postponing the case until it is seen whether a case before a court in another EU or EEA Member State will be rejected or admitted for a full trial on its merits. A Danish court cannot refer a case to a foreign court, and the response is, therefore, rejection (cf. section 248, subsection 2, 3rd sentence).

Referral, which is really a 'service' rendered to the plaintiff, is used in cases where the court has the power to refer rather than apply the more drastic measure of rejection. A case is referred:

47. *UfR* 1991:733 V.

- if the court does not have the professional competence to hear the case, for example, where a city court case is taken to the High Court (cf. section 232, subsection 2);
- where a city court refers a case to the High Court because the court finds that the case raises matters of principal importance (however, the High Court may refer the case back if the High Court finds that this criterion is not fulfilled);
- where the court has no territorial competence (jurisdiction) to hear the case because the case was taken to the wrong city court or High Court (cf. section 248, subsection 2, 1st and 2nd sentences) or;
- where a city court refers to a case, in which knowledge of business relations, including maritime cases and employment cases, to the Maritime and Commercial Court (cf. section 227).

Chapter 2. International Jurisdiction

§1. Rules Applicable in the Absence of a Treaty

83. Under the terms of procedural law, foreigner nationals are:

- persons with foreign domicile and no domicile in Denmark;
- persons who are resident abroad and have no domicile in Denmark;
- persons whose last known place of domicile was not Denmark;
- persons whose last known place of residence was not Denmark.

If the defendant is a foreigner as defined in procedural law and not covered by the Brussels I Regulation discussed below, paragraph 92, he may be sued in Denmark if one of the *Rpl*'s exceptional jurisdictions (cf. above, paragraph 79) can be applied (cf. section 246, subsection 1).

84. If the court of the branch is invoked, it must be remembered that the branch has no independent legal capacity. The moment a foreign company is dissolved, the branch ceases to exist. Thus, in Chevron, a pending employment case against Chevron's branch in Denmark had to be dismissed immediately on the dissolution of Chevron in Delaware, US.[48]

85. Proceedings under property law can be brought in Denmark if, at the time when the writ was served, the defendant was staying in Denmark (cf. section 246, subsection 2). Such a stay can be as brief as a stopover in a Danish airport.

86. A more practical option is the quasi-in-rem jurisdiction (cf. section 246, subsection 3), where proceedings may be brought in Denmark if the defendant had items of value in Denmark at the time when the writ was served. Any asset of financial value can in principle create jurisdiction. A claim constitutes an item of value at the place where the debtor is located according to the claim. A negotiable document constitutes an item of value at the address where the document is kept. The conditions regarding the value of the claim are modest, although a forgotten umbrella or similar would not constitute an item of value. Assets which cannot be taken in execution can also constitute an item of value. There must presumably be some minimum degree of clarity with regard to the value. Neither may plaintiff have employed illegal means in gaining possession of the item of value. A counterclaim can constitute an item of value.

The asset which constitutes the object of a case can constitute an item of value. In *Agilent Technologies, Inc.*, the majority of three justices in the High Court assumed that the sub-sub-sub-subsidiary in Denmark of an American company (i.e., a 'great-great-grandchild company') did not constitute values in Denmark, whereas the dissenting justice rightly pointed to the fact that even subsidiaries further down

48. *UfR* 1989:969 Ø.

in a 'chain' constitute possession belonging to the ultimate parent company. The dissenting justice was obviously right in his opinion.[49] Please observe that the quasi-in-rem venue *cannot* be applied in cases involving the Brussels I Regulation; in such cases, only the different kinds of venue vested in the Regulation are applicable. Consequently, the quasi-in-rem venue is only applicable in connection with other persons or companies domiciled outside Denmark than those comprised by the Regulation.

87. It is important to remember the difference in the meaning of court of performance relative to defendants from the EU Member States and other foreign defendants. Under the Brussels I Regulation, the court of performance also applies in cases of purely financial claims. The foreign contractual partner who should have provided a service in Denmark may, therefore, be sued in Denmark, although the service is simply a financial payment. In cases involving other foreigners under procedural law, however, the court of performance under the Danish rules does not apply to purely financial claims. In *Jørgen Schmidt Trading A/S*, a Danish company wanted to sue its Swedish sole distributor in a Danish court because the Swede had allegedly not observed adequate notice in his termination of the distributorship. The Supreme Court found (dissenting vote 4–1) that although the alleged claim which was to be performed in Denmark was governed by the contractual relationship between the parties, this was nevertheless a financial claim which therefore came under the exemption contained in section 242, subsection 2. The fifth judge agreed that the claim arose from the contractual relationship but did not find that the expression 'financial claim' contained in section 242, subsection 2 should be interpreted so broadly as to include a duty to terminate a contract with a given period of notice, although such a claim will be transformed into a financial claim in legal proceedings.[50]

88. If a vessel is arrested ('frozen'), the main case (including confirmatory action) can be brought to the jurisdiction where the arrest was made (cf. section 246a of the *Rpl*). It should again be remembered that if the Brussels I Regulation applies to the defendant, all jurisdiction provisions, including section 246a, give way to the Brussels I Regulation (cf. section 247, subsection 1). If the ship's owner prevented the arrest by providing security, the case may be brought to the jurisdiction where the arrest should have been made.

89. Proceedings may of course also be brought in Denmark under jurisdiction agreements.

§2. International Treaties

90. After the EU extended its scope to include legal cooperation, the Brussels I *Convention* was replaced by the Brussels I *Regulation*. Denmark was a signatory to

49. In *UfR* 2006:2503 Ø.
50. *UfR* 1992:746 H.

the Convention and has also obtained a parallel convention to the Regulation, bringing this into force in Denmark as from 1 July 2007. Also, the amendments to the Regulation, cf. (EU) 1215/2012 (the 'Recast') apply to relations between the EU and Denmark. In Denmark's case, Greenland and the Faeroe Islands were neither governed by the Convention nor by the Regulation.

91. With effect from 1 July 2017, Denmark is also, through its EU membership, a party to the 'Convention on Choice-of-Court Agreements' established on 30 June 2005 under the Hague Conference on Private International Law (PIL) (Danish: *Værnetingsaftalekonventionen*). The impact of this is double: (1) venue outside EU agreed by the parties in an exclusive choice-of-court agreement is respected by courts in all countries that are parties to the Convention, and (2) judgments pronounced by a court following such a choice-of-court agreement shall be recognized and enforced in all countries that are parties to the Convention.

92. And now back to the Brussels I Regulation and its impact in Denmark. The Brussels I Regulation only applies to civil proceedings. It does not apply to criminal cases (except that it includes ancillary proceedings, i.e., civil claims decided as part of a criminal case). In *Volker Sonntag*, an Italian ancillary judgment in a criminal case against a German teacher was thus able to be enforced in Germany. On a school excursion to Italy for German children and with a German teacher, a boy was killed, and criminal proceedings were taken against the teacher, Volker Sonntag, in an Italian court. The judgment against him was recognized and enforced in Germany.[51]

The whole idea of the Regulation is to facilitate a 'free movement of judgments' in civil cases in all of the EU, confer the remarks from the European Court of Justice (ECJ), in *Unibank v. Flemming Christensen*: 'The purpose is to achieve free movement for judgments by the means of a simple and quick procedure for *exequatur*.'[52]

93. The dominant rule under the Brussels I Regulation is the same as for the *Rpl*, that people must be sued in their home court, i.e., the court of domicile (cf. Article 2, subsection 1). It is irrelevant whether the defendant is a citizen of the country of domicile. Only domicile matters (cf. Article 2, subsection 2). If doubt should arise as to the definition of domicile, the court where the case is brought applies its own definition of the concept (cf. Article 62). A company or similar entity has, of course, no 'domicile'; instead, either its statutory domicile or its head office applies (cf. Article 63).

94. In cases involving contractual relationships, proceedings may be brought where the obligation which gave rise to the case has been or should be performed

51. ECJ judgment in C-172/91.
52. C-260/97.

(court of performance, court of contract) (cf. Article 7, no. 1a), and especially concerning purchase of goods and services, the place of delivery is considered as the place of performance (which is a speciality of the Regulation, compared to the former Convention).

Considering the case law of the European Court and the practical needs of private business, there is no doubt that the court of performance is the most important exceptional jurisdiction by a long way. The court where the case is brought must apply its own PIL rules to decide which country's laws should apply when the court of performance is determined. So the court deliberates in three steps: (1) it applies its own PIL (normally as regulated in the Rome I Regulation) to find the proper law of the contract; (2) it applies the law of the contract to find the place of performance; (3) if the place of performance is in the country of the court, the court has competence in the matter.

As mentioned, the Regulation's court of performance also applies to purely financial claims. This is one aspect of the Regulation which has engendered considerable misunderstandings in Danish courts among other places, at least in the past, as it is foreign to the Danish way of thinking that an unpaid seller can sue in his own court, because the claim for which action is taken, claim for payment, must be performed there (under Danish law, the debtor must deliver money owed, in contrast to most other countries, where money owed must be collected by the creditor). With the Regulation, the place of performance was specified in cases where the contract concerns sale of goods or services, cf. above, and here it is felt more 'natural' that the place of delivery (which is not necessarily also the domicile of the seller) acts as the venue. However, if goods are sold, for example, ex-works, meaning that the place of delivery is the seller's factory, and probably also his domicile, he can sue the purchaser there.

The court of performance causes problems because it is defined by the place of performance for precisely the claim from which the case arose. It was long been felt that there was a need to simplify this court, but the adjustment which was able to gain support is nevertheless rather restricted in scope. Claims involving goods and services may, as already mentioned, now be taken to the court of performance, irrespective of the obligation which occasioned the case. However, other types of contracts are still governed by the Tessili rule,[53] so that proceedings must be brought in the country where the obligation from which the case arose should have been fulfilled. The old case law thus continues to act as a precedent.

Please observe that a contract on the sale of goods, using the term '*franco* ... ', does not necessarily mean that the parties have agreed on the place after '*franco* ... ' as the place of performance, and consequently that this place might not be the venue of performance in the sense of the Regulation. The term will often only mean who is carrying the freight expense to that place, not that the place is also a place of performance, cf. A.T.I. s.r.l concerning delivery 'franco Skanderborg (Jutland)' of some pipes from an Italian seller; this did not constitute Danish venue.[54]

---

53. ECJ judgment of 6 Oct. 1976, C-12/76.
54. *UfR* 2001:1039 H.

95. In some cases, not only the place of performance and thereby also the venue, but also the very existence of the contract, is contested by the defendant, and consequently also the venue emerging from the contract. In accordance with such types of cases, the ECJ has developed the *Effer criteria* prescribing that it does not in itself preclude a venue that the existence of the contract in which the venue is agreed is contested by the defendant.[55] The court has to examine whether such criteria are found present which are characteristic for such kind of contract.

This calls for a preliminary examination of whether a contract would seem to have been entered into. If this is *not* found to be so, the case will have to be dismissed. Cf. *Elodie S.A. 'Les Mariées d'Elodie'* where a Danish undertaking sued a French undertaking, but where the main characteristics of the kind of contract invoiced did not seem to be present.[56] Through such a dismissal, the question of the existence and validity of the contract is not res judicata, but might be tried in another case before another court. If the characteristics are found to be present, the case is admitted, but again is not res judicata that the contract is valid.

The possibility of such a preliminary decision – simply to get over the question of dismissal or admittance, in order to get on with the case – is well known from an arbitral procedure where one also knows the principle of *separability*. *See also Bisgaard & Partnere Fyn ApS* which also applies the concept of separability; it was held that a local manager of a workshop did not have a power of attorney to enter into an agreement on the venue on behalf of his company.[57]

96. The court of performance (venue of performance) is, of course, only applicable if the case concerns a contract, hereby also including liability connected with a contract. If the reason for the case is a liability outside contract, the venue of performance is inapplicable, cf., for example, the ECJ in *Tacconi*, concerning alleged pre-contractual liability.[58]

97. In cases involving compensation outside contract, but not *actions paulienne* or similar, the case may be taken to court in the place where the wrong was committed (cf. Brussels I Regulation Article 7, no. 3), i.e., the court of tort, cf. *Reichert & Kockler and Dresdner Bank*.[59] The court of tort (court of damage/court of a harmful event) can be applied in cases involving product liability. It follows that a manufacturer will often not be able to predict where jurisdiction may be established for actions brought against him for the injurious qualities of his product.

In *J.J. Rooze og Sobema, S.A.*, it was thus established, and doubtless rightly so, that Danish jurisdiction applied in a case against the Belgian seller and the Dutch dealer of a merry-go-round sold to a Danish person who had erected it in the entertainment park *Dyrehavsbakken*, where it caused serious injury to a 13-year-old boy.[60]

55. C-38/81.
56. *UfR* 1998:1092 Ø.
57. *UfR* 2008:2727 Ø.
58. C-334/00.
59. Cf. judgment in C-261/90.
60. *UfR* 1994:342 Ø.

The court of tort may also be applied in transnational defamation cases, although it is important in this type of case to define where the damage primarily occurred as jurisdiction may otherwise be established in several Member States simultaneously.

In *Fiona Shewill and others*,[61] the European Court established that British jurisdiction applied in an action which Fiona Shewill and some companies wanted to take against the French companies which published the *France Soir*. To avoid the potential problem mentioned above, it is essential to distinguish between primary and secondary damage, cf. *Marinari and Lloyd's Bank*.[62]

98. Cases arising from the operations of a branch, an agency, etc., may be launched in the court in the place where the company is situated, i.e., the court of the branch (cf. Brussels I Regulation Article 7, no. 5).

A German lawyer's unstaffed office in Copenhagen which he used occasionally was not a 'branch'.[63] The court of the branch does not depend on compliance with the conditions governing the court of performance. The obligation which gave rise to the action must, of course, be commercially linked to the branch, but it need not have its place of performance in the Member State in which the branch is located cf. *Lloyd's Register of Shipping*.[64]

99. If several persons are sued in the same case and only one of them is sued in his home court (but not in an exceptional jurisdiction), the other defendant(s) can be sued in the same court, i.e., cumulative jurisdiction (cf. Article 8, no. 1) if, for example, several suppliers are sued in the same case on product liability.

100. The consumer can sue the provider of goods or services in the consumer's own state if the purchase was by credit buying or in response to advertising, etc., in the consumer's home state (court of the consumer) (cf. Articles 17–19). It will be seen that the scope of the Regulation's consumer jurisdiction is somewhat broader than that of the Danish (cf. section 244 of the *Rpl*). The court of the consumer lapses, however, if the consumer's claim is transferred to a commercial entity and no longer pursued by the consumer in person: cf. *TVB Treuhandgesellschaft and the brokers Hutton Inc.*[65]

101. Jurisdiction agreements may be entered into provided there is no obligatory court (i.e., no sole competence applies under Article 24, immovable property) (cf. Article 25).

See on this *Investorgruppen Danmark K/S 14* et al.,[66] *Texpro* et al.,[67] *Scan-Expo Hans Wortmann GmbH*,[68] *Oskar Schunck KG*[69] and *SP Massivbau-System*

61. C-68/93.
62. Cf. C-364/93.
63. Cf. *UfR* 1991:52 Ø.
64. C-439/93.
65. C-89/91.
66. *UfR* 1990:597 H.
67. *UfR* 1991:245 SH.
68. *UfR* 1992:886 V.
69. *UfR* 1995:725 H.

GmbH.[70,71] Jurisdiction agreements may also be entered into tacitly by appearing in court without objection (cf. Article 26, subsection 1). On this, *see Pic Pic/Unicopa* for a very liberal interpretation of the defendant's obligation and duty to launch a preliminary objection in the first plea.[72] The dissenting opinion appears more correct.[73] If a jurisdiction agreement can be tacit, it can naturally also depend on custom and commercial practice, cf. *Custom Made Commercial.*[74] In *Mankowski*, the court had the opportunity of providing a somewhat more specific answer to the question of what it takes for a jurisdiction agreement to have been informally established between commercial partners.[75] The court stated that a jurisdiction agreement can be entered into: (a) by remaining passive towards the other party's jurisdiction provisions in the printed text to which an order confirmation refers, and even (b) by repeated payment without comment on invoices containing the jurisdiction clause, provided, however, that it is established usage that agreements can be made informally in this area of business and that the parties are aware of it. A clause conferring jurisdiction in a company's statutes is also valid in the sense of the Brussels I Regulation (cf. *Powell Duffryn plc v. Wolfgang Petereit*).[76]

102. Counterclaims may be brought during the main proceedings (cf. Article 6, no. 3). A Danish submission to the court resulted in a more precise formulation of the counterclaim concept: in a case of a claim which would require an independent judgment, i.e., not merely a claim for compensation, which is really little more than a defence, the court has independent competence under the Regulation to decide the claim. Otherwise, the claim must be rejected.

In *Danværn Production A/S,*[77] the court stated that Article 8, no. 3, only governs counterclaims submitted for independent judgment. The provision thus does not apply to situations where a defendant merely claims as a point of defence that he has a claim against the plaintiff (counterclaim for compensation). Consequently, a claim which a (Danish) defendant brings against a (foreign) plaintiff's main claim must be considered only a point of defence if it has no content other than compensation.[78]

This state of law is logical, but not without problems, as the court's decision with regard to a counterclaim made purely in defence also has the force of law. The court can, therefore, find itself in a position where it makes a decision which has the force

70. *UfR* 1996:937 H.
71. Cf. Ketilbjørn Hertz in *UfR* 1997 B, 43 et seq. On international jurisdiction agreements, *see* particularly Leif Weizman in *TfR* 1992:656 et seq.
72. *UfR* 1993:792 V.
73. *See also* Ketilbjørn Hertz in *UfR* 1997 B, 43 et seq. and Jensen & Arnt Nielsen in *UfR* 1994 B, 287 et seq.
74. C-288/92.
75. C-106/95.
76. C-214/1989.
77. C-341/93.
78. *UfR* 1996:13 V. The city court had therefore been wrong in rejecting the claim under the terms of Art. 6, no. 3. The city court's rejection of the case was consequently overruled, and the case was remitted to the city court for continued hearing.

of law with regard to an unconnected claim, which the court would not be competent to judge under the terms of the Regulation.[79]

103. The Regulation and its uniform application must not be made illusory through various national provisions, typically aimed at extending the competence of the national courts and restricting the competence of courts in other signatory states. Perhaps the most essential element in relation to traditional Danish jurisdiction clauses is the Regulation's barring of quasi-in-rem jurisdiction, which it deems to be exorbitant. Neither can the court's international competence be made illusory through an anti-suit injunction, although such means of redress may exist in national procedural law, cf. *West Tankers*.[80]

79. Cf. Reinhold Geimer in *EuZW* 1995:640 et seq.
80. C-185/07.

Part III. Actions and Claims

Chapter 1. Actions

§1. Definition

104. The Danish Rpl does not define the concept of legal proceedings as such but merely states when civil proceedings have been commenced, i.e., upon submission to a court of a writ (cf. section 348 of the *Rpl*).

The right to take legal action does not depend on the existence of a particular type of writ (*actio*) covering the precise type of claim. The right to take action is independent in principle of substantive rights, and no matter how much the defendant feels that the case instigated against him is unfair and unfounded, he has to defend himself.

Danish civil procedural rules do not know, e.g., the English concept of *strike-out* or *anti-suit injunction*; i.e., the defendant cannot obtain a fast and swift decision that the case against him must immediately be dismissed. However, at the end of the case, it will be clearly shown how the court's view on the case is; if the court finds that the case was unjustified from the very start, this will result in a decision from the court that the plaintiff must carry the costs of the case. An anti-suit injunction is, for cases where the venue is regulated by the Brussels I Regulation, considered to be contrary to this Regulation, cf. *West Tankers*, because anti-suit injunction rulings disturb the distribution of competences between the courts in the EU.[81]

§2. Admissibility

I. Cause of Action: The Party's Specific and Current Interest in Having a Case Tried

105. The cause of action concept, understood as a specific and current interest in having a case tried, serves as a barrier, the purpose of which is to discard matters which are not so well explained and documented that they ought to be admitted to a court hearing. There are no written rules, but a lot of case law, in Denmark to determine 'cause of action' in any general sense, and the meaning of the concept as applied to the admission or rejection of writs, therefore, depends on theory and practical experience.

81. C-185/07.

In *Jan Rosberg*, a taxpayer had attempted to jump the standard complaints system provided in the Tax Administration Act, as he wanted an early answer to the question of whether some new changes in the tax law also applied in his case. The case was, however, rejected by the courts, as the taxpayer's interest in obtaining speedy clarification of the effect of the new provision on his loans did not set him apart from other taxpayers who were forced to await the usual process through the tax system before being able to obtain a final decision on their problem in court. The Supreme Court added that there were no 'such special circumstances' in relation to the case as to justify a full hearing, irrespective of the Tax Administration Act's special rules on when a case could be taken to court. In other words, the court did not definitively exclude the possibility that in certain circumstances such special cause of action could exist.[82]

This does not necessarily mean that a disagreement which is no longer current lies outside the court's competence.

See on this *Flemming Juncker*, where, as the case was an offshoot of a specific earlier disagreement, the Supreme Court admitted a declaratory action from an A shareholder against the company's biggest B shareholder, in which the A shareholder claimed that the company's statutes should be interpreted to mean that a general meeting was able to decide to redeem the B shares, without the B shares being able to take part in the vote on the question.[83] *See* further below, paragraph 109, on declaratory actions.

106. However, an actual interest which has existed might have vanished if the case is no longer of any significance to this or other parties' legal position, cf. *Praktiserende Arkitekters Råd*, where a project for a public tender – which was probably unlawful on certain points under public procurement law – was now definitely given up, and compensation had been paid to all undertakings having spent time on the matter.[84]

The lawfulness of measures taken pursuant to criminal law may also frequently be tested after they have ceased.[85]

107. If the defendant unconditionally has paid full compensation to the plaintiff but has indicated that he does not feel legally obliged to do so, the plaintiff has under Danish procedural law no actual interest in a case against the defendant only to have established by court that the defendant was obliged to pay what he has already paid.

This was seen in the tragic case where the family of young victims of an accident on the Roskilde Festival were suing the association behind the festival.[86] The association had paid the full amount demanded by the families without any kind of condition, only indicating that the association did not feel legally bound to do so. The

82. *UfR* 1995:265 H.
83. *UfR* 1958:90 H.
84. *UfR* 2004:3051 H.
85. Cf., e.g., *UfR* 1996:1468 H, where the Supreme Court tested the lawfulness of some cases of telephone bugging. The rights injured by measures such as those involved in this case were so vital in the eyes of the court that the plaintiff possessed the requisite interest in having their lawfulness tried, although the event lay well in the past.
86. *UfR* 2007:2161 H.

families returned the money, but the association confirmed that it would at any time be ready to pay the amounts again (and it was undoubtedly able to pay). Nevertheless, the families wanted a case against the association to have the liability for the tragic accident clearly shown, but both the High Court and the Supreme Court found that the families had no actual interests in such a case, and accordingly the case was dismissed from the courts.

II. The Distinction Between Deciding a Specific Case and Writing a 'Legal Opinion'

108. Judges do not write general opinions on hypothetical questions of law but decide a particular dispute which has arisen between two or more parties based on documentation presented on the parties' mutual manner of acting, negotiations, etc.

However, some case law contains cases almost approaching an expert opinion-producing activity on the part of the courts. These cases have involved parties who were in general disagreement on points of law but had no concrete case to take to the courts (as agents for members).

See The Trade Union HK v. The Association of County Councils in Denmark on the interpretation of the 120 days absence from work rule in the Salaried Employees Act in the event of partial absence.[87] The case was admitted on a 5-4 dissenting vote. In borderline cases such as this, it is essential that the case be made as specific as possible and fully documented to the court. Otherwise, it must be rejected.[88]

In the *HK Trade Union*, the union wanted the Association of County Councils ordered to recognize that a county council must be deemed to be the 'same undertaking' in relation to the Salaried Employees Act. The Supreme Court gave as grounds for its rejection that the case could involve highly diverse employment conditions within individual counties and that it would hardly be possible to examine these differences in the course of the action in such a manner that an adequate basis could be established for deciding HK's 'generally worded claims'.[89] The key issue was thus again whether the case was concrete and fully documented to the court.

In *HK Denmark*, the trade union HK sued a large Danish employers' association (*Dansk Arbejdsgiverforening*, DA) with the aim of obtaining a judgment ordering DA, within its fields of competence, to secure that equal salary for men and women be paid, and to establish statistics segregated by gender for Danish business undertakings. The Supreme Court found that even if a duty to establish such statistics might be concluded from the relevant EU Directive, such duty did not apply to all undertakings regardless of size, collective agreements, etc. The court proceedings did therefore not allow to establish a sufficient basis for HK's claim which was formulated in rather general terms.[90]

---

87. *UfR* 1990:611 H.
88. Cf. Torben Jensen in *UfR* 1986 B, 406 et seq. and *UfR* 1990 B, 441 et seq.
89. *UfR* 1994:60 H.
90. *UfR* 2007:213 H.

After the insurance group Hafnia had collapsed, and cases of prospectus liability were pending, an accountant brought action before the special Board of Accountants (*Revisornævnet*) against Hafnia's accountants, but the Supreme Court agreed with the board that it was not enough for the plaintiff to be – as he put it – 'professionally concerned' about the case; he lacked actual interests in the case, and his case was rejected.[91]

A case which has been 'constructed' in order to obtain the courts' view on a hypothetical legal question must be rejected.

In EU law, *see*, e.g., *F.A. Meyer AG*,[92] where a member of a company and its management had 'constructed' a dispute masked as a question by the shareholder to a general meeting on the extent to which a capital increase obtained through the conversion of a loan must be treated as a cash or a non-cash contribution under company law.

109. The general assumption is that the right to take legal measures is conditional upon the person requesting the measure having a specific legal interest in doing so. The cause of action is thus often both a written and a tacit condition supplementing other conditions. For example, any person possessing the requisite interest in law can obtain information on the processing of a deceased estate from the probate court or the administrator of the estate (cf. section 114, subsection 2 of the Administration of Deceased Estates Act). Declaratory proceedings and bankruptcy petitions can only be submitted by persons with the requisite interest, although this is not stated in any rule of law. A bankruptcy petition submitted by a creditor who would clearly gain no dividend at all from the procedure because, for example, his claim is subordinated (liable loan capital) must be rejected, and so must a petition from a creditor whose claim is undoubtedly secured by mortgage, bank guarantee, etc.

The cause of action concept is used in many quite different contexts, and its content typically varies with the context. An example is a party's capacity to sue and be sued, which may be absent if the plaintiff is not the person to whom the claim involved would revert.

See, e.g., *Løkken Strandgård A/S*, in which a shareholder believed that he had suffered a loss because the company's bank had followed unlawful instructions from the company's managing director to use the company accounts to the personal advantage of the director. Neither the city court nor the High Court found that the shareholder who held 50% of the share capital while the managing director held the other 50% had the capacity to sue, as no contractual relations existed between the shareholder and the bank, and the case could not be deemed to concern a violation of a shareholder's individual interests.[93]

110. In the case testing, the constitutionality of Denmark's accession to the EU Treaty, the Eastern High Court applied a precedent which had emerged over the years and which stated that single persons who are not individually and directly

91. Cf. *UfR* 2003:5 H.
92. C-83/91.
93. *UfR* 1992:780 V.

affected by law cannot take legal action to test its compliance with the Constitution. The case law then current did not acknowledge a person's civil status as a citizen of Denmark to constitute an adequate legal interest in the case. Probably under some influence from the constitutional courts of other nations, the Supreme Court decided, however, in a historic judgment that in this particular case at least, the requisite interest was present.[94]

The court stressed the following elements: (1) the Treaty involved the transfer of legislative competence within a range of general and essential areas of life of vital importance to the Danish population in general; (2) this set the case apart from other cases intended to test the constitutionality of particular pieces of legislation; (3) because of the general and vital importance of the Accession Act, the plaintiffs had a material interest in having their claims tested; and (4) given these facts, it was not necessary for the eleven plaintiffs to document that legislation had been issued pursuant to the Union Treaty which had a concrete and current effect on their lives. The case was then remitted to the High Court for a full trial.

III. Class Actions

111. With effect from 2008, Danish procedural law allows for class actions. Following recommendation no. 1468/2005 by the Standing Committee on Procedural Law, the possibility of class actions with effect for cases brought on or after 1 January 2008 was introduced into Danish law.[95]

Under section 254b, subsection 1 of the *Rpl*, class actions can be brought when:

(1) there is a common claim as specified in section 254a;
(2) there is a venue for all of the claims in Denmark;
(3) the court is the venue for one of the claims;
(4) the court possesses the requisite expertise to deal with one of the claims;
(5) class actions are judged to be the best manner of handling the claims;
(6) the members of the class can be identified and informed of the case in an appropriate manner; and
(7) a class representative as per section 254c of the *Rpl* can be appointed.

Condition number 5 in particular – that the class actions are judged to be the best manner of handling the claims – is intended as an estoppel against wild and groundless actions. The court must accept in each individual case that a class action is more appropriate than traditional rules on subjective accumulation.

---

94. *UfR* 1996:1300 H.
95. *See* on this matter Erik Werlauff, *Class Actions in Denmark*, in *The Globalization of Class Actions* vol. 622, 202–208 (R. Deborah Hensler, Christopher Hodges & Magdalena Tulibacka, eds, The Annals of the American Academy of Political and Social Science March 2009). Also *see* Erik Werlauff, *Class Action and Class Settlement in a European Perspective*, European Business Law Review 173 et seq. (2013).

If the court does not possess the expertise to handle all claims under an independent case, it can refer the case for decision in a court with the expertise to handle at least one claim under section 254b, subsection 2 of the *Rpl.*

112. Under section 254c of the *Rpl*, class actions are conducted by a *class representative* on behalf of the class. The class representative is appointed by the court. The representative may be: (1) a member of the class; (2) an association, private institution or other organization when the action falls within the framework of the organization's object; or (3) a public authority authorized for the purpose by law, for example, the Consumer Ombudsman.

In class actions under section 254e, subsection 8 of the *Rpl*, i.e., actions under the *opt-out* arrangement, the only eligible class representative is a public authority authorized for the purpose by law.

The Consumer Ombudsman can be appointed class representative in a class action under section 35 of the Danish Marketing Practices Act, section 348, subsection 1 of the Danish Act on Financial Activities, section 120, subsection 1 of the Danish Investment Association Act and section 3, subsection 3 of the Danish Securities Trading Act.

The class representative must be able to look after the interests of the class members during the case.

113. Under sections 254d and 348 of the *Rpl*, class actions are brought by *submitting a writ* to the court. The writ can be submitted by anyone who can be appointed a class representative under section 254c, subsection 1.

Apart from the normal requirements for writs under section 348 of the *Rpl*, the writ in a class action must also contain: (1) a description of the class; (2) information on how the class members can be identified and informed of the case; (3) a proposed class representative who is willing to assume the task.

114. The court appoints a class representative if there is compliance with the terms in section 254b and c for bringing the case as a class action under section 254e. The court can decide in connection with the appointment of the class representative, or after the expiration of the deadline for joining or withdrawing from the class action, that the class representative must provide security for the legal costs which the representative may be required to pay the opposite party. The nature and extent of such security are decided by the court. If the security is not provided and another class representative is not appointed, the case is rejected.

The court can subsequently *appoint a new class representative* if required. In class actions under the opt-in procedure under subparagraph 6, the court must decide whether it is necessary to appoint a new class representative if at least half of the class members who have joined the class action so request, and the request is accompanied by a proposed new representative who is willing to undertake the task.

115. The court *sets the framework for the class action.* The court can subsequently alter the framework if so required.

116. The class action covers the *class members who have joined the action*, i.e., an *opt-in* procedure, unless the court decides that the class action must cover those members of the class who *have not withdrawn from* the action, i.e., an *opt-out* procedure. It has generally been found that an opt-out is foreign to Danish legal thinking, and an opt-out, therefore, requires the presence of quite special circumstances and as noted, only a public authority can serve as the class representative in opt-out actions.

Opt-in: the court specifies a deadline for joining the class action by written submission. The court decides to whom notice of joining is to be given. In exceptional cases, the court can permit joining after the deadline if there are extenuating circumstances.

The court can decide that joining the class action is conditional upon the member's providing *security for legal costs* specified by the court unless the member has legal aid insurance or other insurance which covers the costs of the case, or the class action fulfils the terms for free legal aid under sections 327–329 of the *Rpl*, and the member fulfils the financial conditions under section 325 of the *Rpl*. The Minister of Justice advises on application from the class representative whether the class action fulfils the terms for free legal aid under sections 328 and 329.

Opt-out: if the class action concerns claims where it is clear that *the claims cannot be expected to be made in individual actions because of their small size* and it can be assumed that a class action with opt-in would not be an appropriate manner of handling the claims, the court can decide on application by the class representative that the class action will cover those members of the class who have not opted out of the action.

In this event, the court specifies a deadline for opting out of the class action by written notification. The court decides to whom the notification should be given. In exceptional circumstances, the court can permit opting out after the deadline if there are special reasons for doing so.

Common features of *opt-in* and *opt-out:* those persons whose claims fall within the framework of the class action must be informed of the above terms and the legal effects of opting in or opting out of the action. This information is provided in a form specified by the court – *see* below, paragraph 124, on the probable significance of contact over the internet. The court can specify that the notification be made in whole or in part via public announcement. The court can require the class representative to carry out the notification. The costs of the notification are paid in the first instance by the class representative.

117. The class representative and the class' opposite party are considered *parties to the class action* under section 254f of the *Rpl*. In particular, this entirely new concept of 'party' in procedural law had required a lot of consideration before Denmark was in a position to introduce rules on class actions.

118. The court's decisions in a class action have a *binding effect on the class members covered by the action*. With respect to decisions on counterclaims, this applies, however, only to claims arising from the same contract or the same facts on which the class members' claim is based. In class actions under section 254e, subsection 8 of the *Rpl*, the court's decisions only have a binding effect on class members who could have been sued in Denmark for the claim in question when the case was first brought.

119. A class member can be *ordered to pay legal costs* to the opposite party and/or the class representative, but such that the opposite party's claim takes precedence over that of the class representative. The class member cannot, however, be ordered to pay legal costs over and above the amount specified under section 254e, subsection 7 of the *Rpl*, i.e., the security provided plus any sum owing to the class member as a result of the case.

To the extent to which legal costs awarded against a class member who complies with the financial terms under section 325 of the *Rpl* are not covered by legal aid or other insurance, *the costs are paid by the state* if the class action fulfils the terms for free legal aid under sections 327–329, but at a maximum calculated according to section 254e, subsection 7.

This is intended to avoid an outcome like that described in *Scan Detectronic Production*,[96] where 254 private persons attempted via a class action to gain release from their participation in a limited partnership which had been offered to the public, but which proved to follow a course entirely different from that which had been expected. Both the Maritime and Commercial Court and the Supreme Court of Denmark to which the case was appealed upheld the limited partners' liability, and they were ordered to pay costs to the opposite party (a bank which had had the limited partnership's claim to the remaining liability transferred to it from each individual limited partner). For the individual partner, one or more DKK 50,000 shares were involved – but the 254 losing partners were ordered to pay legal costs of DKK 600,000 in the first instance and DKK 800,000 in the second instance – i.e., a total joint liability of DKK 1,400,000 – to test whether they were liable for the remainder of the subscribed sum of DKK 50,000 in court. Irrespective of the material result of the case, such an outcome – and such a gigantic risk for the individual limited partner in the legal action – is obviously totally unsatisfactory.

Other Danish cases also indicate that the ordinary rules of procedure, including those on subjective accumulation and legal costs, must often capitulate in the face of the facts. Many shareholders who had suffered losses after the collapse of a Danish insurance company thus attempted to claim against the failed insurance company's management, auditors and issue bank via two associations created for the purpose, but the associations' action was denied by the courts because the formation of associations without personal liability is deemed to constitute a circumvention of the rules on legal costs under Danish law, cf. *Hafnia*.[97]

120. If the question of *cancelling or dismissing the class action* arises, the class members who are parties to the action must be notified unless notification is clearly superfluous under section 254g of the *Rpl.*

96. *UfR* 1996:271 H.
97. *UfR* 2000:575 H.

The court may decide on notification in other situations, including in the event that a settlement proposal comes up for approval.

121. If a class action is cancelled or dismissed, a class member who is party to the action can *intervene* by written notification to the court within four weeks *and continue the case under the rules for individual actions insofar as the member's own claim is concerned.* The same applies if the court decides pursuant to section 254e, subsection 4, no. 2 that a particular claim is not covered by the class action.

122. Any settlement entered into by the class representative on claims covered by the class action becomes valid when the settlement is approved by the court under section 254h of the *Rpl.* The court will approve the settlement unless the settlement discriminates against some class members or is otherwise patently unfair. Class members who are parties to the action must be advised of the court's approval of a settlement.

The court advises the class members who are parties to the action of the result of the case under section 254i of the *Rpl.* On request, the court sends a transcript of the proceedings to class members who are parties to the action.

123. If a judgment in a class action is appealed by the class representative, section 254e, subsections 5–9, similarly applies as per section 254j, i.e., the rules on party status, etc., also apply in the appeals case.

If the class representative does not appeal, any person who is eligible for appointment as the class representative under section 254c, subsections 1–2, can commence an appeal. If the class representative appeals part of a judgment, the same rule applies to those parts of the judgment which were not appealed.

If the opposite party appeals a judgment in a class action, the appeal is heard in accordance with the rules on class actions.

A class member who is party to the action and whose claim is not covered by an appeal under section 254j can appeal a judgment in a class action under section 254k insofar as it relates to the member's own claim. Any appeal or petition to appeal is deemed to be made in time if the notice of or petition to appeal is submitted within four weeks of the expiration of the normal deadline.

124. Leading Danish lawyers with considerable court experience are prepared to handle class action cases. The large legal chain Ret & Råd, which comprises more than seventy legal firms throughout Denmark, has registered the domain names http://www.enfaellessag.dk ('a common case') and http://www.viermange.dk ('we are many'), and the big legal firm Nielsen & Nørager has registered the name http://www.gruppesøgsmål.dk ('class action'). Contact with clients via the internet is a crucial factor in the practical handling of class actions. The role of the media in informing about contemplated and pending class actions will also be of importance.

125. The provisions on class actions had effect as from 1 January 2008, and already in that same month, the first Danish class Action was taken to court and recognized by the city court and the Eastern High Court as a class action. It was a claim from a large number of shareholders in a bank in bankruptcy, *Bank Trelleborg*. The class action is not about board members' liability, but litigation brought against a larger bank, *Sydbank*, and against the Danish Financial Supervisory Authority (*Finanstilsynet*), because the shareholders in Bank Trelleborg were subject to redemption of their shares after the bank had suffered heavy losses.

In 2015, the collapse of the stock-listed Danish company OW Bunker, which collapsed only seven months after the Intellectual Property Organization (IPO) where it was introduced on the Nasdaq OMX Copenhagen, seems to have caused a number of class actions against merchant banks, accountants and board members, perhaps even against the sellers of the IPO introduced stocks.

126. A party may fail to prove the cause of action because he has no legal capacity about his own case. This is the situation if, for example, the case is governed by a collective agreement so that the right to take legal action falls to his trade union's legal system. If, however, the trade union refuses to take the case, basic legal rights, including the right to have one's case tested in court (cf. Article 6 of the EHRC), guarantee that his personal legal capacity is reawakened: cf. *Gert Tonny Hummer*, which ruled that a trade union member whose organization refuses to pursue a potential claim for wage compensation through industrial arbitration possessed the capacity to take the case to court in person.[98]

The Supreme Court stated that the provisions of the Employment Act compared with the EHRC's Article 6, subsection 1 must be understood to mean that an employee whose trade union does not want to pursue a wage claim in connection with a dismissal is not prevented from taking legal action in the courts in person. It was irrelevant to the case whether the claim was based on a collective agreement or other law. Both the city court and the High Court (2-1) would have rejected the case, but the five judges on the bench in the Supreme Court agreed that it should be admitted. The right of employees who are not members of a union to take legal proceedings has been recognized for many years (cf. *Villert Orla Sørensen*,[99] *Kirsten Christoffersen*[100] and *Jan Finn Petersen*).[101]

§3. Vexatious Litigation

127. When a case has been brought, it must proceed through the exchange of pleas, trial hearing, etc., unless there are grounds for rejecting it or it is settled amicably out of court.

Danish procedural law does not recognize the concept found in some other countries, for example, The UK, where a court can order the case to be struck out; such striking-out orders are not possible under Danish law. Regardless of how strongly the defendant may experience the case as 'unfair' or 'groundless', neither the court nor any person other than the plaintiff can release him from an action which has been admitted, merely because it appears a hopeless case on the part of the plaintiff.

98. *UfR* 1994:953 H.
99. *UfR* 1985:800 V.
100. *UfR* 1985:997 Ø.
101. *UfR* 1987:406 Ø.

A private person who has been sued must, therefore, live with the financial and psychological uncertainty caused by a pending case.

A business owner finding himself taken to court must similarly consider what effect this may have on the annual accounts while the case is pending, including whether allocation should be made in anticipation of loss or a note should be attached. The parties will only receive an indication of whether the court considers the case to be lost after the completion of procedure in the first instance, and the definitive knowledge comes with the judgment passed in the case unless an out-of-court settlement is reached.

If the court finds that the case should not have been brought, this may be reflected in the costs and, in very few cases, in the plaintiff's legal counsel being made jointly liable for the costs pursuant to section 319 of the *Rpl*: cf. *Teddy Mørch*,[102] which makes a lawyer jointly responsible with his clients (some limited partners) for groundless legal proceedings brought against a bank. The bank's lawyer had several times drawn the plaintiffs' lawyer's attention to the fact that the claim against the bank was groundless. Before 2005, the court could order a fine for vexatious action, but this possibility was removed from Danish procedural law because it was applied extremely seldom.

128. Some countries have provisions for banning legal action, i.e., a way of preventing a case from continuing, or even the launching of an announced case, either because it is evidently baseless or because the court in which it is launched lacks the competence to hear it (i.e., another court than the one issuing the ban). An example is the anti-suit injunction in British procedural law. Such an order cannot be issued by a Danish court, and recent case law from the ECJ shows that an anti-suit injunction is not compatible with the Brussels I Regulation, cf. *West Tankers.*[103] Through such an injunction, the division of competence between the courts in the different EU countries would be distorted.

102. *UfR* 1999:99 H.
103. C-185/07.

Chapter 2. Claims and Defences

§1. Definition

129. A party's claim is, in concentrated form, a statement of the outcome the party wants the case to have, for example, that the defendant must pay a certain amount of money to him with interest accruing in a particular manner.

The claim is formulated such that it can be inserted in the judgment without amendment – if the party making the claim wins.

130. The plaintiff's claim could, for example, be:

(1) A claim for payment formulated to be inserted practically verbatim into the judgment if the plaintiff succeeds in the claim. The claim may have the following wording: 'THAT defendant DD be ordered to pay DKK 500,000 to plaintiff PP, plus ordinary pre-judgment interest from the instigation of the case until payment is effected.' And the final judgment may be: '*THI KENDES FOR RET:* … IT IS HELD THAT: Defendant DD shall pay DKK 500,000 plus ordinary pre-judgment interest from the instigation of the case until payment to plaintiff PP is effected.' Such a claim is a petition to the court to pronounce an enforcement order which the plaintiff can ask the bailiff's court to enforce if the defendant fails to pay.

(2) A declaratory claim formulated to be inserted into a declaratory judgment. The claim may be worded as follows: 'THAT defendant DD be ordered to recognize that defendant's publication of a plant catalogue entitled "Plant Catalogue Spring 2009" was unlawful in relation to plaintiff PP.' The final judgment may repeat this verbatim – if the plaintiff wins. Apart from any costs awarded, a declaratory judgment is not enforceable as such, but if judgment creditor (plaintiff) holds the title to a piece of chattel held by judgment debtor (defendant), the judgment can form the basis of immediate enforcement proceedings (so-called possession proceedings) in which the bailiff repossesses the object upon request from judgment creditor, as the declaratory judgment has created the requisite clarification. A declaratory claim does not state why it was made (*in casu*: why defendant's publication of the catalogue is unlawful in relation to plaintiff). The reasons for this are not stated in the claim, but explained in plaintiff's presentation of the facts of the case and later in the grounds of the judgment (reasoning) if the claim succeeds.

131. The defendant's claim can be:

(a) A guilty plea, i.e., defendant defends the plaintiff's claim (a concept which laymen often find difficult to grasp). A guilty plea may be given if the parties agree on one or more of the plaintiff's claims. If, for example, a plaintiff both claims a declarative judgment that defendant's action was unlawful and an enforcement order with regard to a payment claim, the defendant may choose to defend the declaratory claim, but to contest the claim that any loss for which he was responsible was thereby caused. In a divorce case, the defendant may defend the claim that the parties be granted divorce or separation while contesting the claim regarding custody of children, alimony, etc.

(b) A 'blank' not guilty plea, which of course occurs very often. Put in writing in the defence (or orally during the initial hearing) it simply states: 'acquittal of defendant'.

(c) An alternative plea for payment of a smaller amount. This is routinely formulated as 'acquittal against payment of a smaller amount than claimed by plaintiff' – although this would clearly not be an acquittal, but rather a judgment pronounced. The tradition of formulating such an alternative plea in this illogical way has been criticized in Danish jurisprudence, but it seems impossible to get rid of it, and everyone knows what such a plea means.

(d) A counterclaim, which must state whether it is merely made as a point of defence (*modkrav til kompensation*, counterclaim for compensation) or submitted for independent judgment (*modkrav til selvstændig dom*, counterclaim for independent judgment). In the latter case, a court fee is payable as for a claim in a writ, and the value of the case – and the costs to be carried as well as the entire risk involved in the case – are increased correspondingly. A counterclaim made as a point of defence can merely result in a claim for complete or partial acquittal, as it is regarded only as an allegation made by the defendant. A good description as to how not only Danish procedural law but also EU law and procedural law in most other countries look upon the difference between the two kinds of counterclaims can be found in the ECJ judgment already mentioned – *Danværn Production*,[104] where the question at stake was the competence of the court according to the Brussels I Regulation (then the Convention on 'counterclaims').

132. During the course of the proceedings, each party is normally given three or four opportunities for specifying its claim: (1) during preparation of the case, i.e., in the exchange of pleas contained in the parties' writs; (2) possibly in a separate defence document submitted prior to the full hearing, as the court can now request submission of a written plea with a summary of allegations, list of documentation, etc.: cf. now section 357, that may be sanctioned with default judgment; (3) at the start of the oral hearing when the claims are repeated; (4) during the opening of the party's final oral arguments, where it is customary, although not explicitly ordered, that the barrister repeats his party's claim (in order to make sure that the hearing has not given his party cause to waive any part of his claim).

As already mentioned, it is a very important principle in civil procedure, perhaps the most important one, that the court cannot award a party more than what he claims (cf. the principle of party presentation in section 338 of the *Rpl*). This maxim is based on the principle that the parties define the issues of the case. The claim, therefore, constitutes the upper limit of what that party can win through the court case. This is another point which sets the civil procedure apart from the administrative law's inquisitorial procedure.

---

104. C-341/93.

§2. DISTINCTIONS

133. Plaintiff can submit one or more alternative claims in case he fails to succeed in his principal claim, for example, 'THAT defendant DD be ordered to pay DKK 500,000 to plaintiff, alternatively a smaller amount as decided by the Court.' The grounds on which the alternative claims are based are not stated in the claim but will appear in the allegations. An alternative claim is by definition less far-reaching than the primary claim. If the primary claim is upheld by the court, the court will of course not consider the alternative claim.

A claim for formal rejection of the case should always be made as the primary claim over a claim for acquittal. Of course, cumulative claims can also be submitted, for example, that plaintiff claims both that a house transaction be cancelled, and that compensation be granted, possibly combined with alternative claims for a smaller amount for compensation than stated in his primary claim.

134. Counterclaims can be made even if the main claim and the counterclaim should in principle be processed using different procedures, for example, as proceedings before a housing tribunal and before an ordinary court.

Cf. *APV Pasilac A/S*, where a commercial property was sold for DKK 64 million and leased back to the seller, who then promptly made a claim to a housing tribunal for reduction in rent and repayment of rent. As counterclaim to the claim for compensation, the buyer wanted to claim a proportionate reduction in the purchase sum. In contrast to the High Court, the Supreme Court found that he was entitled to have this counterclaim decided in relation to the question of compensation under the rent case.[105]

The claim made by the lessor was conditional upon the lessee succeeding in his claim for a reduction in the rent, and the court supported the lessor's claim that he might forfeit his legal rights if the claims, which were both financial claims, were not decided together.

If the defendant makes a claim that requires independent judgment, it is an indication of a wish that several claims be heard during the same case, i.e., so-called objective, passive accumulation. Defendant can make his counterclaim during the case, even if, on starting a separate case on his counterclaim, he could not have taken it to the same court because of the jurisdiction rules (cf. section 249, subsection 2, of the *Rpl*). If, on the other hand, the case involves the court's international competence under the Brussels I Regulation and the counterclaim is submitted for independent judgment, the claim must either be connected, i.e., arising from the same legal relationship as the main claim, or the court must possess independent competence under the Regulation to hear the counterclaim.

Cf. Article 6, no. 3, of the Regulation as interpreted by the European Court in *Danværn Production A/S*,[106] cf. the Danish decision derived therefrom.[107] On the one hand, a counterclaim constituting merely a point of defence can always be

105. *UfR* 1993:657 H.
106. C-341/93.
107. *UfR* 1996:13 V.

heard; on the other hand, irrespective of whether the court would possess independent competence to do so under the Regulation's rules of jurisdiction, as such a claim is merely an allegation in support of acquittal and therefore falls outside Article 6, no. 3. This state of law is logical but, as already pointed out, not without its problems, as the court's decision about a counterclaim made as a point of defence also has a certain binding effect. The court may, therefore, end up deciding an unconnected counterclaim with binding effect, which it would not have geographic competence to decide under the Regulation.[108]

135. Case materials also comprise, apart from the parties' claim/defence, allegations (*anbringender*) and documentation. Allegations are statements and considerations presented by a party with regard to the facts and law of the case.

Plaintiff's allegation is called *søgsmålsgrunde*, cause of action. This is the substantive basis on which the claim is made, particularly the legal grounds – such as agreements, wrongful acts, property rights, instruments of debt or guarantees. In this terminology, the word 'argument' is used in a 'loose' sense to cover considerations and statements in support of the claim. The *Rpl* uses only the term 'arguments', thus subsuming cause of action.

The defendant's arguments are called *indsigelser* (objections or points of defence), and the terminology is thus complete: the plaintiff's allegations or causes of action (*søgsmålsgrunde*) are countered by the defendant's allegations, objections or points of defence (*indsigelser*), and together the causes of action respectively the objections constitute the allegations of the case (*anbringender*).

136. A distinction is made between points of fact and points of law. The parties' only obligation is to present the facts for the court's deliberation. In principle, it is then the court's duty to apply the law to the facts on its own initiative, as in principle the judge has a general duty to know valid Danish law. As far back as Roman procedural law, this was expressed in the motto: *Narra mihi factum, narro tibi jus.* In other words, the judge's statement to the parties or their lawyers is: Tell me the facts and I will tell you the law. Or in even more succinct terms: *Jura novit curia*, i.e., the court knows the law.

In practice, however, it may sometimes be difficult to distinguish between law and facts. A point of fact can at times be incomprehensible or meaningless except in the context of law. Although the parties have no duty to present points of law, they may of course do so, and they will often have a keen interest in touching on the law in the case in order to influence the court's decision. It is therefore common for the counsels in representing the parties to provide the court with references to jurisprudence, case law, etc., which support their stand in the case, and the court is always ready to listen if the points made are relevant to the case.

In cases where complicated law is involved, it is common for the advocates to establish a 'collection of materials' (*materialesamling*), in which photocopies of relevant jurisprudence, case law, deliberations by the Parliament when treating a bill, etc., are contained. If possible, advocates should establish a common collection of

108. Cf. Reinhold Geimer in *EuZW* 1995:640 et seq.

materials. The court cannot order the advocates to establish a collection, but advocates often do so on their own to facilitate the judges' preparation prior to the oral hearing.

Factual allegations are documented through evidence. No proof can be presented regarding the law, but proof can be presented with regard to (trade) practices, customs and foreign law. Judges are not obliged to know the content of a particular custom or tradition. The question of whether foreign law is seen as a point of fact which the parties must present and document, or as a point of law which the court must in principle have knowledge of, or procure knowledge of, has changed over time.

The current tendency is probably more or less to consider foreign law analogous to Danish law, but this does not mean that the parties are not welcome to provide information to the court on foreign law, for example, through the presentation of copies of jurisprudence and case law.

The general tendency under Danish procedural law to consider foreign law as a part of *jus* in the case is parallel to what can be detected in other countries, cf., e.g., German *ZPO* section 293, which states that foreign law is considered part of *jus*, and only needs evidence to the extent that the court does not know the contents of foreign law.[109] It has also been established in tax cases that foreign law needs no evidence, and that survey on foreign law (here: Lithuanian law) is excluded.[110]

It is also possible to present a legal opinion from a foreign lawyer, but as such opinions can often not be given or read independently of the concrete facts of the case; it will often be best if the parties procure them jointly if the intention is to submit them during the case. There has been a restrictive attitude in Danish case law regarding the submission of legal opinions on Danish law prepared by professors and other expert lawyers, cf. *Blåvandshuk Kommune*.[111]

However, in *Telekæden A/S*, the Supreme Court took a new path, now holding that such *legal opinions may be submitted to the court for the sake of the legal argumentation, but not as a proof.*[112] This new and refreshing attitude has opened the way to an ever-deeper argumentation from each of the parties on the legal aspects of the case. As part of a reform suggested by the Danish Civil Justice Council in report no. 1558/2016, it has been codified (*Rpl* section 341a, subsection 2) that legal opinions on Danish law may be submitted to the court for the sake of the legal argumentation, but not as a proof.

Allegations (*anbringender*) can also be described as the connecting link between the facts of the case and the parties' claims. An allegation can therefore also be said to be the justification for the claim made. The court justifies the final judgment (*THI KENDES FOR RET:* ..., IT IS HELD THAT ...) in a set of premises or grounds (e.g., 'The court finds that ... '). The parties justify their claims with one or more allegations ('It is alleged that ... ').

An allegation typically comprises both fact and law and is structured in two parts, one containing the presentation of an event, and the second a legal framing of it.

109. *See* Rainer Hausmann, *Pleading and Proof of Foreign Law - a Comparative Analysis*, European Legal Forum 1, I-1 et subs (2008).

110. Cf. *TfS* 2008:1364, city court.

111. *UfR* 1996:1293 H, with critical commentary by Lennart Lynge Andersen & Bernhard Gomard in *UfR* 1997 B, 231 et seq.

112. *UfR* 2014:138 H.

If, e.g., the plaintiff claims compensation from a parent company for the losses a creditor has suffered through the bankruptcy of a subsidiary of that parent, it is necessary to formulate the allegation (however short) in such a way that the facts are closely connected to relevant law: *Primarily*, defendant DD (the parent company) is liable for the plaintiff PP's (the creditor's) loss because the defendant on the [date 20xx] issued a guarantee against such loss. *Second* (if letters, etc., from the defendant cannot be understood as a guarantee, but perhaps merely as a letter of awareness), the defendant is liable for the plaintiff's loss because the defendant through its behaviour acted with negligence. *Third* (if no guarantee and no negligence can be demonstrated), the defendant must be held responsible on grounds of 'piercing the veil', based on case law.

Chapter 3. Sanctions on Procedural Irregularities

§1. Formal Requirements

137. If the plaintiff's writ fails to fulfil the requirements of section 348 of the *Rpl*, and therefore fails to provide an adequate basis for processing the case, and if the defect is not remedied within a given period, which the court may set, the case will be rejected (cf. section 349, subsection 2 of the *Rpl*). The case is also rejected if the plaintiff fails to appear at the final oral hearing.

In a lease case, the court found the writ in a case on the termination of a lease because of breach of contract to be so inadequate that the case was rejected. The writ stated that the lease was terminated because of breach of contract, but the nature of the breach was nowhere indicated, not even indirectly in the annexes provided.[113]

138. After having received the plaintiff's writ, the court lets the writ serve to the defendant unless the court knows that the defendant is represented by a counsel who will, on behalf of the defendant, waive to have the writ served and instead receive the writ in an informal way. The court admits to the defendant a certain time limit (not less than two weeks, in practice often somewhat longer). Within this time limit (which may be prolonged, for example, if the defendant has had difficulties in finding a counsel to represent him, and the counsel has only had very little time to deal with the case), the defendant has to submit his writ of defence to the court and to the plaintiff (*Rpl* section 351).

If the defendant fails to do so within the time limit set by the court, the court pronounces judgment in accordance with the claims of the plaintiff, *insofar* as the court can see from the summons and the annexes attached to it that the claim is justified. There have been cases where it was obvious to the court that, for example, the plaintiff's claim for interest could not be justified, and in such cases, the court only pronounces a judgment which the court finds justified, i.e., the claim for interest might be cut down or dismissed.

Please note that the consequences of the defendant's failure to respond within the time limit set by the court are different in court cases than during arbitral proceedings. During an arbitral proceeding, the defendant's (respondent's) failure to respond does not constitute any kind of waiver on his side, and the arbitral proceedings will have to continue with documents, evidence, arguments, etc. On the contrary, a court proceeding will not have to continue in such a situation; instead, the court pronounces, as already mentioned, a judgment in accordance with the claims of the plaintiff, insofar as the court can see from the summons and the annexes attached to it that the claim is justified.

139. One of the issues of the Court Reform 2007/2008 was to secure that the preparation and hearing of the case are, at the soonest possible stage, agreed in

113. *UfR* 1997:1120 Ø.

detail between the court and the parties. The instrument to secure this is a preparatory meeting (*forberedende møde*, cf. *Rpl* section 353), which after the reform plays a significant role in speeding up civil cases. The meeting is often held between the court and the advocates, but the advocates must before the meeting make sure, e.g., that they have a good grip of their party's calendar, because one of many items at the preparatory meeting is, if possible, to fix the date for the final oral hearing of the case (*hovedforhandlingen*, the final oral hearing).

The preparatory meeting ('the section 353 meeting') may be held as a phone meeting, where some or all parties attend by phone. This concept has been shown to function very well, and it is, of course, time-saving for all parties involved.

Section 353 contains a long list of items which will, if relevant to this particular case, have to be discussed at the meeting. Some of the items are:

- On which points do the parties agree, and on which points do they disagree?
- Can we already now fix the date for the final oral hearing? If the answer is yes, please consult your calendars now, and let us fix the date.
- Are their objections as to any formalities?
- Would the parties like the case to be heard by three professional judges (instead of one, which is the main rule)?
- Would the parties like two expert judges to hear the case (together with one or three professional judges)?
- Would it be relevant to refer the case to the High Court as the first instance (because the case is of principal importance)?
- Would we have to postpone the case to obtain a preliminary ruling from another instance, for example, from the ECJ?
- Are there any procedural 'provocations' which the parties would have to deal with, for example, a request for certain documents which one party urges the other party to submit?
- Would a survey be necessary, and if so, how do we find the right person(s) as surveyor(s)?
- What costs (not in every detail, but in broad lines) will this case cause?
- Will it be relevant to obtain written witness statements?
- When, and how time-consuming, will the final oral hearing be?
- Will it be relevant to try to obtain an amicable settlement between the parties (such questions always being discussed 'without prejudice' to the parties claims and allegations if a settlement is not reached)?
- Will it be relevant to try some kind of alternative dispute resolution (ADR), e.g., Court Mediation (*retsmægling*) offered by all Danish city courts after the reform (of course, again 'without prejudice' if an amicable settlement is not reached)?

As it will be seen from this, one does only have to cast a glance at section 353 in order to obtain a good idea of the whole procedure for the preparation and hearing of a civil case in the first instance (but, of course, all the points mentioned are not relevant in all cases; they exist as a mere catalogue of inspiration for the meeting).

140. Hopefully, the case is on good and firm tracks after the preparatory meeting according to section 353, but it is possible to hold further preparatory meetings (*Rpl* section 355), also as phone meetings. This may be relevant in cases where the court and parties have to discuss how to conduct a survey in the case, for example, how to find the right person(s) as surveyor(s), possible objections from one party to the questions the other party wants to ask the surveyor(s), etc.

The questions are basically formulated by the parties, but if they disagree on questions as the correct formulation, or what documents must be submitted to the surveyor(s), etc., the court will have to hear the arguments, to try to obtain a settlement on this formal question, and finally to decide this question if no mutual understanding is obtained. Finally, on one such preparatory meeting, the date for the final oral hearing must be fixed – and thus the discussion of the points mentioned under section 353 is completed. The idea is, again, that the court and the parties should know, at the earliest possible stage, when the final oral hearing is to take place.

141. After the preparatory meeting, according to section 353, the preparation of the case usually continues with one further writ from each side, exactly as it is well known from the procedural law in other countries, i.e., the rebuttal (*replik*) and the rejoinder (*duplik*). Although the *Rpl* gives the impression that the court can allow such further writs, the parties would probably be highly surprised if the court denied them the right to do so; rebuttal and rejoinder are in practical life more the main rule than the exception. However, further writs than those four already mentioned will be an exception, for example, if a survey has been carried out, and both parties need to comment on the results of the survey, perhaps even to change their claims.

142. The preparation of the litigation is completed when the court so decides (*Rpl* section 356). If no specific decision is pronounced by the court, the preparation is per definition completed at the date exactly four weeks before the date which has been fixed for the final oral hearing. The *Rpl* attaches great importance to the date where the preparation is completed. The party's claims and allegations can freely be changed, also augmented, until this date, but after this date, changes in claims and allegations (apart from pure waivers) are subject to certain conditions. One could say that the claims and allegations are 'frozen' on this date to make it possible for both parties and the court to prepare for the final oral hearing. If a party wishes to change his claims or allegations, he must obtain the acceptance of the other party to do so, or he must, failing acceptance from the other party, persuade the court that he should be allowed to make such changes. If the court receives such a petition, the court must take into consideration whether the party has a reasonable ground for the petition, and failing such reasonable ground, the court must consider the impact on the party's case, if his petition is dismissed, in other words: how important is it to him to be allowed to change his claims or allegations? If the court allows him to do so, the other party must under all circumstances be given due time and possibility to prepare himself for the new situation; if necessary, the date for the final oral hearing must be postponed.

§2. Time Limits

143. The writ of defence from the defendant must be submitted to the court within the time limit fixed by the court, and the time limit must at least be two weeks, in practice often somewhat longer (*Rpl* section 351).

The *Rpl* contains no specific time limit for the preparatory meeting according to section 353, so the court decides discretionarily on this matter, however often after having consulted both parties per phone.

144. In civil proceedings, witnesses are entitled to one week's notice when summoned; in criminal cases, only 'one night's notice' (+ forty-eight hours for witnesses living more than 30 km away from the courtroom) (cf. section 175, subsection 3). Normally notices are much longer, however, because of the delay between the issuing of proceedings and trial. The court can decide a shorter notice or order a witness to appear immediately (cf. section 175, subsection 4), which is sometimes important in practical terms if explanations are given in a criminal case during the full trial which requires the calling of a particular person as a witness.

In civil matters, witnesses are usually in practice not summoned by the court but have agreed with the party who wants to hear the witness that the witness is able and willing to appear at that certain time when the party estimates that the time has come during the oral hearing to hear this witness. Of course, if a witness cannot be reached by such an agreement, the party will have to ask the court to summon the witness, and a subpoena summoning the witness will then be served on the witness.

Please again observe that the Court Reform 2007/2008 created the formal legal basis for applying written witness statements (cf. *Rpl* section 297), either where the parties agree or where the court permits the use of such statement because the court finds it unproblematic. However, as already mentioned, the use of written witness statements does not at all have a proportion under Danish law as we know it under, e.g., US or UK procedural law, or as we know it from ICC or LCIA arbitration proceedings.

Written witness statements will remain an exception under Danish procedural law. It is suitable for witnesses who are by no means 'main witnesses' of the case, and where the need for cross-examination does not exist. A written witness statement is not a supplement to oral evidence from the witness, but that the written statement replaces the oral evidence.

145. The court must make its decision in civil cases 'with all due speed after the trial has ended', and when the case is set down for judgment or order, the court must indicate when the judgment or order will be given (cf. section 219, subsection 1, 1st sentence, of the *Rpl*). City courts must hand down a judgment or order not later than four weeks after the case has been set down for judgment if the case is heard by a single professional judge. The time limit is two months in city court cases with three judges, and also two months in High Court cases. These limits may, however, be extended in special cases (cf. section 219, subsection 2). In criminal cases, the judgment must be given 'with all due speed after the trial has ended', and the dominant principle is that if judgment cannot be given on the same day, it should follow within a week at the most, in trial by jury not later than the following day, cf. section 219a, subsection 1.

Part IV. Proceedings

Chapter 1. Pretrial Proceedings

146. There is no obligatory conciliation or mediation phase preceding legal action in Denmark. The party that decides that negotiations are futile is free to decide to take legal action. Neither is it necessary to document to the court that everything possible was done before proceedings were brought to settle the case amicably. On the contrary, it may in some circumstances be contrary to sound legal practice if a lawyer discloses in court what proposals were made to settle the issue without prejudice to the case by one of the parties during earlier negotiations.

This is not to say, of course, that negotiations before a court case play no practical role in the Danish administration of justice. They most definitely do but based on tradition and custom and not as ordered by law. However, pursuant to the Court Reform 2007/2008, *offered* by law, i.e., as it was seen above, paragraph 139, under the mentioning of the preparatory meeting, every city court in Denmark does now, as a regular part of the preparation of cases brought before the court, offer the parties a Court Mediation or: ADR, for example, Court Mediation (*retsmægling*) offered by all Danish city courts after the reform (as already mentioned: 'without prejudice' if an amicable settlement is not reached).

The 'standard' fee for court mediation (*retsmægling*) conducted by one of the authorized mediators attached to the courts, often local practising lawyers, would be DKK 8,740 + VAT. If the mediation lasts more than approximately five hours, the fee will be increased by DKK 1,790 + VAT per additional hour (Tariffs as per 1 January 2021 as agreed upon by the presidents of the High Courts, available at the website http://www.domstol.dk).

If for no other reason than the time and cost factor, it will often be entirely natural for parties who disagree on the interpretation of an agreement, for example, to seek to settle the case before taking legal action – and pursuant to the Court Reform 2007/2008 the court will often encourage to try such ADR, and the court will offer experienced mediators at a fixed price per hour. Any hope by the parties of being able to continue their contractual relationship in the future normally also points clearly in this direction. Many agreements between business people contain explicit provisions to the effect that bona fide negotiations must be undertaken before either party proceeds to take legal action, i.e., a mediation clause (concepts for which might also be found on the web pages of most arbitration institutions).

If the parties disagree on their mutual legal rights and obligations, negotiations aimed at an amicable out-of-court settlement of the case play an important practical and litigation-saving role. A common reason for mediation is if one party believes that the other party owes him an amount of money under the terms of a contract, or because of a breach of contract, and the other party denies owing the money or the full amount, and both parties recognize that there is a risk for both of them attached to any legal action being taken, and that this risk plus time and cost considerations favour an attempt to reach a settlement, even if this means departing somewhat from one's principles and starting point.

147. Settlement negotiations can be time-consuming, and they may end in no result for the party counting on receiving payment. If the debt believed to be owed is not already accruing interest, either because this was agreed or because the date of payment was agreed in advance, and if he is not satisfied with being paid pre-judgment interest from the date when the case was launched, as is the main rule under section 3, subsection 4 of the Act on Interest (*renteloven*), he should be advised to make a request for interest payment at an early stage during the mediation phase (cf. section 3, subsection 2). If he does so, his claims will carry interest starting thirty days after the request.

Compared to what you meet in other countries, where interest on court or arbitral claims is often, for example, 5% yearly, the interest rates emerging from the Danish Act on Interest are rather high, varying with one of the interest rates fixed by the Danish Central Bank (Nationalbanken, Denmark not being member of the Euro countries, but having its currency locked firmly to the EUR).

A Danish Justice of the Supreme Court, often acting as arbitrator in international cases, likes to tell a story about some complicated arbitral proceedings where he was one of the arbitrators. The three arbitrators had a number of vivid discussions concerning the claimant's different claims which the arbitrators were inclined to reduce considerably. Especially the American arbitrator hesitated in this reduction, but when he learned how much the interest accrued according to the Danish Interest Act would increase the total amount that the award would bring the claimant, he was relieved – and highly surprised.

If a writ is later issued in the case, the plaintiff must remember to include interest from this early date in his claim for interest payment, as interest claims are also governed by the doctrine contained in section 338 – the principle of party presentation – stating that the court cannot award a party more than he has claimed. It follows from this that one should recommend the creditor whose claim is contested and who hesitates in bringing the case to court that he sends a request for interest, cf. section 3, subsection 2 of the Act on Interest, and that he, if the case is brought to court, naturally remembers in his summons to make a claim for interest, cf. *Rpl* section 338. Thus, both the substantial legal basis for interest and also the procedural legal basis for awarding him interest together with his main claim are present.

148. It may happen during mediation that each side offers a non-committal proposal (a settlement proposal 'without prejudice', *forligstilbud uden præjudice*) on how the case might be settled.

It is regarded as contrary to sound legal practice if, in a later court case, a lawyer reveals or documents that the other party was willing to settle the case in a particular manner at an earlier stage.[114] It should not be deemed to be a 'sign of weakness' if a party and his lawyer make a sincere attempt at establishing a basis of agreement.

A different situation from such non-committal proposals arises if a party simply offers one solution. In a dispute between two ex-cohabitants, for example, the defendant had before the litigation offered to pay DKK 25,000 to the plaintiff, and the outcome of the process was a judgment of – DKK 26,250. Hence, the true winner of the case was the defendant, and he was awarded DKK 10,000 as legal cost.[115]

Somewhat more particular about the precision of the pretrial offer is a case concerning two groups of heirs in a deceased person's estate, where the High Court quoted the report leading up to the Court Reform that if the losing party did not offer sufficient (one penny less, as they say in the UK), such a non-committal proposal has lost its importance. Even if it was a committal proposal – but still 'one penny less' than what was actually owed – such proposal can only lead to a minor reduction in the costs that the losing party will have to refund to the winning party. On this background, the Court of Appeal found that the losing party would have to pay costs calculated on the total amount which had been claimed and won from him.[116]

149. If mediation ends in a settlement, it means that the parties have ended the case themselves by entering into an agreement. The parties are free to settle the claim, and hereby also free to settle whether interest and costs, etc., must be paid, as there is freedom of contract for all dispositive cases. Rather often, part of a settlement may contain a clause that each party carries his own costs, and perhaps also that the demand on which the parties agree is paid without interest – but as mentioned the parties are free to settle such matters exactly as they wish.

The question of legal costs is often left for the court to decide, and there has been some doubt whether the parties are free to appeal such a separate cost decision if their settlement is silent about this specific matter. In *Bisgaard & Partnere ApS*, the Supreme Court ruled that failing an agreement by the parties to waive their possibility of appeal, each party is free to appeal the cost decision separately.[117]

If the debtor is willing to sign an out-of-court ('voluntary') settlement (*udenretligt forlig*), but cannot pay all at once, and if the creditor is willing to accept an instalment scheme, the latter can be built into the settlement agreement before signing. If the repayment period exceeds three months and the debtor is a consumer while the creditor is a businessman undertaking and/or represented by a lawyer, the out-of-court settlement is then governed by the rules of the Credit Agreement Act (*kreditaftaleloven*), which is again governed by an EU Directive, and it follows that more detailed information must be given to the debtor on the loan capital, credit

114. Cf. on the approximately similar position in Swedish law, Lars Heumann in *SvJT* 1991:87 et seq., who points out, however, that the ban only covers lawyers and their representatives, but not, of course, the parties themselves.
115. *UfR* 2008:129 H.
116. *UfR* 2010:597 Ø.
117. *UfR* 2008:926 H.

costs, annual costs in percentage and total amount for payment, the size, number and payment date of the individual payments, the term of the agreement, and conditions for its termination.

Lawyers undertaking debt collection have calculator functions built into their word processing systems for complying with this duty to inform before the signing of the settlement. When a lawyer issues a filled-in form for a voluntary settlement, it is normally clear from the text that the creditor reserves his approval of the instalment scheme. It follows that the form does not constitute an offer, but an invitation to make an offer.[118] The duty to inform under the Credit Agreement Act therefore only became effective from the time of the creditor's acceptance.

150. One of the main purposes of such a settlement has been to form a basis on which execution may be levied on the debtor in case of breach, without the creditor first being required to take out a writ and obtain judgment against him. If an out-of-court settlement is to serve this function, the settlement must state explicitly that it can serve as a basis for execution (cf. section 478, subsection 1, no. 4 of the *Rpl*). The relevant clause may state: 'This settlement may serve as the basis for an execution' ('*Dette forlig er eksigibelt*'). A petition for execution cannot be made until the so-called days of grace have expired (cf. sections 484 and 486). Unless otherwise agreed, the period of grace for out-of-court settlements is fourteen days counting from the due date for payment. Another period may be agreed, but it may not be shorter than four working days (banking days). It may, therefore, be useful to state in the settlement that the period of grace is four working days.

Please observe that another possibility of avoiding costly court proceedings in order to obtain a fundament for execution has existed under Danish law since 2005, i.e., through the concept of execution on the basis of a Demand for Payment (*betalingspåkrav*), cf. *Rpl* section 477a. The main conditions are that the claim does not exceed DKK 100,000 (approximately EUR 13,300) and that the debtor does not contest the claim. If the claim is contested, the creditor will have to take his case to court as in other civil proceedings, cf. section 477f.

118. Cf. *FM* 1993:131 V, where the creditor reserved his acceptance of the agreed instalment plan and where the agreement was not deemed to have been entered into until the creditor had given his acceptance.

Chapter 2. Proceedings in First Instance

§1. Adversary Proceedings

I. Ordinary Proceedings

A. *Introduction of the Claim*

151. Legal action commences with the submission of a writ (*stævning*) to the court (cf. section 348 of the *Rpl*). The court fixes a deadline for defendant's submission of the statement of defence (*svarskrift*).

152. When suing a general partnership, it is not necessary to state who the partners are, cf. *Amfa I/S*.[119] If, however, a judgment is sought not only against the partnership but also against the partners in it personally, they must be named, not only as partners ('General Partnership X owned by the general partners ... ') but also as co-defendants. When suing a limited partnership, it is also unnecessary to name, e.g., the partner with limited liability unless judgment is also sought against the partner, cf. *Copenhagen International Hotels K/S*.[120]

In most cases, but not necessarily in all, the writ is prepared by a lawyer on the plaintiff's behalf. There is no requirement that the writ must be submitted on a standard form (cf. section 348, subsection 5), but it must contain the following information (cf. section 348, subsection 2), the following numbers being used here for practical reasons, not being identical with the numbers in section 348:

(1) *Plaintiff's name and address.* If a plaintiff is a legal person in the form of a private or public company, a commercial enterprise or a commercial trust, its registration number with the Danish Business Authority (so-called CVR-Number or SE-number) should be given, but it is not required by law.
(2) *Defendant's name and address.* A defendant must necessarily be one or more natural or legal persons.
(3) *The court where the case is launched.* Plaintiff cannot, on the other hand, indicate what deadline will be given for the submission of the statement of defence because this date is fixed by the court when it has received the plaintiff's writ.
(4) *Plaintiff's claim* (*påstand*). If interest is an issue, it is important to make it part of the claim. Interest payment will only be awarded if it is included in the claim. If more than the usual amount is claimed in prejudgment interest, the justification for this must be given in the Particulars. On the other hand, court costs should not be mentioned in the claim.
(5) *A detailed presentation of the facts and law on which the claim rests*, i.e., substantiation of the claim. This part of the writ is normally titled Particulars (*Sagsfremstilling*), and contains an account which may be quite brief, for example, in cases concerning failure to pay for goods and services provided,

119. *UfR* 1993:601 Ø.
120. *UfR* 1996:1435 Ø.

but in cases on complicated questions of liability for damages, company law cases, etc., must necessarily often contain a chronological presentation of events. The *Rpl* indicated until some years ago that the Particulars have to be 'short', but today the demand is that the Particulars be 'detailed' (*udførlig*). Particulars must (again: contrary to what was demanded some years ago) state not only the facts but also the law, i.e., a reference to the legal allegations (*anbringender*) on which the plaintiff intends to rely.

> If an agreement is invoked, it is, logically enough, not necessary to state that agreements are binding (cf. section 1 of the Act on Contracts). But if it is claimed that an agreement is unfair and therefore *not* binding, it is, of course, relevant to add, for example: 'pursuant to section 36 of the Act on Contracts (*aftaleloven*)'– section 36 being the provision that gives legal basis for annulling or changing unfair contract terms in whole or in part.
> In some cases, the facts are so closely interwoven with the legal arguments that they must be given for the facts to be comprehensible.
> Thus in a case concerning faults in immovable property, it is necessary to know before the end of the pretrial hearing to what extent: (a) the plaintiff believes that the defendant has guaranteed a given quality of the building; (b) the defendant has acted with negligence so as to incur liability for damages; and/or (c) the fault is so extensive that the basis exists for a proportionate reduction in price according to case law on such serious faults.
> There have been cases where the plaintiff remembered to include point (a) and (b), but not point (c), in his allegations, and in such situations, the plaintiff will lose his case if at the end of the day, the court finds that: (a) there is no guarantee and that (b) there is no negligence on the part of the defendant. No matter how strongly the court might feel that the conditions for (c) are present, the court cannot on its own initiative go into allegations connected with (c), cf. again *Rpl* section 338 on the principle of party presentation (*forhandlingsmaksimen*).
> When reading a judgment in a case of some complication, the opening account of the case's main issue, the *narratio*, is often a summary of parts of the writ and the parties' opening addresses during the trial.

(6) *Indication of the documents on which the plaintiff intends to rely*. As for the documents, this is normally done both by inserting an underlined reference to the documents at the relevant points in the Particulars ('*jf. Bilag 1, kontrakt af* … ', ' … cf. Annex 1, Contract as of … '), and by ending the writ with a list of annexes, numbered and with a brief description. All annexes must be attached to the writ unless they have been substantively cited in the writ. If there is a document which the plaintiff does not have and which he thinks is important for the case, he requests the defendant in the writ to produce it: cf. below on requests for further and better particulars (in Danish the so-called procedural provocations, *processuelle provokationer*) and the other party's duty of discovery (please note that failure to comply with the requirements concerning the plaintiff's documents and other kinds of evidence *cannot* lead to the rejection of the case, cf. section 349).

(7) *Indication of other evidence on which the plaintiff intends to rely*. The writ ends with an enumeration of the names (and positions) of the parties and witnesses whom the plaintiff wishes to hear; if he already at this stage knows that he will demand a survey, this must also be indicated. Of course, it may be difficult at this early stage to assess what witnesses may be relevant, and a liberal approach must necessarily be tolerated. Please note again that failure to comply with the requirements concerning the plaintiff's documents and other kinds of evidence *cannot* lead to the rejection of the case, cf. section 349.

(8) *Indication of a postal address in Denmark where letters can reach the plaintiff*, and where documents can be served, normally the plaintiff's lawyer's address.

(9) *The plaintiff's suggestions as to the preparation of the case*. This demand for at further point in the plaintiff's writ came into section 348 in connection with the Court Reform 2007/2008, because there are a number of options to be dealt with, cf. above under paragraph 139 on the very important preparatory meeting to be held when the court has received both the plaintiff's writ and the defendant's statement of defence, cf. section 353 about this meeting. The suggestions concern the following five points: (1) Does the plaintiff suggest that the case be heard by three judges (instead of just one), cf. section 12, subsection 3? (2) Does he suggest that the case be heard also by two expert judges, cf. section 20? (3) Does he suggest that the case be referred to High Court as the first instance, cf. section 226? (4) Does he suggest that an employment case be referred to the Maritime and Commercial Court, cf. section 227? (5) Does he suggest a preparatory meeting to be held, cf. section 353? Please note that failure to comply with the requirements concerning the plaintiff's suggestions *cannot* lead to the rejection of the case, cf. section 349.

153. *If* the writ fails to fulfil the above requirements (apart from the one on indication of documents and other kinds of evidence, and also apart from the one on indication of the plaintiff's suggestions as to the preparation of the trial), and *if* the writ is accordingly unsuitable as a basis for testing the case, and *if* the faults are not remedied within a period of grace which the court may set, the case will be rejected (cf. section 349, subsection 2 of the *Rpl*).

If the defendant moves address after the case has been launched, the case continues in the same court, as the deciding element in determining the defendant's domicile court (and other valid jurisdictions) is the address where the defendant lived at the time when the case was launched.

154. When the case is launched, the so-called lis pendens effect (*litispendens*) applies. *Lis* means legal action and *pendens* means pending. Lis pendens is used to express the rule, however unregulated by written law in Denmark, that when a case on a certain matter between certain parties is pending in a Danish court, no identical case can be taken to the same or another court involving the same cause between the same parties, not even in cases where the second court would be competent under the rules of jurisdiction, for example, because it fulfils the conditions of an exceptional jurisdiction.

The lis pendens effect applies from the start of the action until the expiry of the ordinary deadline for appeals, upon which it is replaced by the so-called cause of action estoppel (because the judgment makes the question decided upon in the judgment res judicata), which has practically the same content as the lis pendens effect. Lis pendens and force of law (res judicata) are thus two sides of the same coin.

155. With the adoption of the Brussels I Regulation, the lis pendens effect applies throughout the EU. An effective lis pendens is an important element in the establishment of the free movement of writs, the free movement of judgments, and hence a *European legal zone* in terms of procedural law, cf. Article 29 of the Regulation. According to Article 32, legal proceedings are deemed to have been launched when the opening document (in Denmark: a writ) has been filed with the court, provided that the plaintiff does not subsequently fail to take the steps required of him to have the document served on the defendant. If national procedure requires that the document is served before it is filed with the court, the case will be deemed to be launched when the document has been filed with the authority responsible for its service, provided that the plaintiff does not subsequently fail to take the steps required of him to have the document filed with the court. It is of great importance that a common lis pendens concept has been adopted through the Regulation, and also that the Regulation – contrary to the Convention – defines a common community concept of when the case has been instigated, and thus when the lis pendens effect takes its start.

B. Progress of Proceedings

156. When the court has received the writ, it is served on the defendant by the court (cf. section 350), unless the court knows that defendant is represented by a counsel who on behalf of the defendant waives to have the writ formally served. A guide is delivered with the writ advising the defendant on what steps he should take to protect his interests as a defendant in a civil lawsuit.

The case is 'filed' when the writ has been served on the defendant. The filing of a case entails – just as in other countries – a number of procedural consequences.

Before the Court Reform 2007/2008, the main rule was that the defendant presented his points of defence orally to the court, but after the reform, the defendant has to submit a statement of defence (*svarskrift*) to the court and to the plaintiff within a time fixed by the court, not shorter than two weeks, often somewhat longer. If the defendant is not represented by counsel, the court may give him an opportunity to elaborate orally on his defence in a preparatory meeting, so the defendant retains his right to explain his case to the judge orally, also during the initial stage.

157. The court can decide, commonly at the time of notification of the initial hearing, that an oral answer is insufficient, and that a written defence must be produced at the hearing (cf. the *Rpl* section 351, subsection 5, 2nd sentence). This is particularly relevant when the court can see from its initial review of the writ that the case is complicated and/or concerns large sums of money.

Instead of reviewing the case in one or more pretrial hearings, the court can decide that it must be heard in writing (cf. section 352 of the *Rpl*), so that a written defence must always be submitted, and no initial hearing is held apart from the section 353 hearing mentioned above, paragraph 139, which must normally be held in order to plan the case. A written hearing is often not something the court plans regarding an individual case, but a general decision applying to most civil cases brought before it.

158. Defendants' statement of defence (*svarskrift*) must contain the following information (cf. section 351, subsection 4 of the *Rpl*).

The documents submitted by the defendant are usually given letters A, B, C, etc. If the alphabet is not sufficient, the defendant continues with AA, AB, etc.:

(1) *The defence claim*, for example, denial of liability, perhaps alternatively 'acquittal against payment of a smaller sum as decided by the court' (which of course is *not* an acquittal).
(2) *Any counterclaims if submitted for independent judgment.* There should be an associated claim for interest. A separate court fee is payable for the counterclaim, and the consequences in costs should not be forgotten.
(3) *An account of facts and law on which the claim and counterclaims if any, are based*, i.e., not a completely new account (a new set of Particulars), but partly a correction of the factual events described in the plaintiff's writ and which defendant challenges, and partly an indication of the most important facts and points of law in support of defendant's claim. Is usual to use the words: '*Supplerende sagsfremstilling*' (supplementary particulars) as a headline for this part of the defendant's statement of defence.
(4) *An indication of the documents and other evidence on which defendant intends to rely.* While the documents (attached to the defence) are important, care is not always taken to indicate as early as the defence what witnesses, etc., will be called, but if the defendant wants an expert appraisal (survey) or expert opinions, it is important to state this.
(5) *An indication of a postal address in Denmark* where letters can reach defendant and documents can be served, often care of defendant's legal counsel.
(6) A very important element in the defence is often the requests for further and better particulars which require a plaintiff to do something or other, for example, release information or produce documents, etc. Cf. more on this question of 'procedural provocations' paragraphs 14 and 139 above.

159. Writ and Defence (with rebuttal and rejoinder: *replik* and *duplik*, together called by the more neutral term 'pleadings', *processkrifter*) are important documents, and the parties have often written everything of importance to the case in them. It is nevertheless possible to continue the exchange generally with another two, or in some cases even another four, documents.

Such further writs have no specific 'names' under Danish law, and they are often simply called 'plaintiff's supplementary writ I', 'defendant's supplementary writ I', etc. ('*sagsøgers processkrift I*', '*sagsøgtes processkrift A*', etc.). In practice, it is the main rule rather than the exception for the parties to exchange rebuttal (*replik*) and rejoinder (*duplik*). This is felt to be so firm a tradition among lawyers that the plaintiff's lawyer will normally say that he 'waives rebuttal' if he does not want to continue the written exchange after having received the statement of defence.

The court sets deadlines for the submission of rebuttal and rejoinder. A request can be made for an extension to these deadlines, and this often happened in the past, with the result that the initial hearing of a case could be drawn out to an unreasonable degree. Today, courts are and must be somewhat stricter when a party wants an extended time limit for his next writ in the case.

If the defendant wants to have the case rejected, for example, because of objections to the competence, venue, etc., of the court, such objections must be raised in the statement of defence.

160. Even the exchange of pleadings is structured on the principle that each party must have the opportunity of familiarizing himself with the other party's point of view and of expressing his own view regarding it. This is the so-called right of defence principle, or the contradictory principle (*kontradiktionsmaksimen*), which (also) plays a focal role in procedural law. This principle is also evident when questions are asked of an expert appraiser (a surveyor) when the case is presented in court, when a witness is examined, and when the parties (or their legal counsels) give their final address.

While the case is under review, the parties must necessarily give careful consideration to the question of which party carries the burden of proof of what is the case, and these considerations should be reflected in the steps taken by the parties with regard to evidence during the review.

Unless, as an exception, it is necessary to produce evidence before an alternative court, for example, because a witness is living abroad or is in very bad health, the immediacy principle dictates that witnesses not be examined until the full trial. Although both the Writ and the Defence must indicate what 'other evidence' (i.e., apart from the documentation), each party intends to rely on, they only decide who to call close to the date of the trial.

A different situation applies where some kind of expert opinion, for example, a survey, must be provided with regard to a state, an event, a service or whatever. Such an opinion can normally not wait until the trial but must be obtained beforehand to allow it to be documented during the trial, possibly supplemented by an examination of the expert in question, a so-called verification.

In cases pending before the Supreme Court, witnesses and parties are heard through separate witness hearings (one might say: witness depositions) conducted before the final oral hearing. The Supreme Court does not hear parties or witnesses directly, and instead, such evidence is taken before trusted clerks of the Supreme Court (*Rpl* section 4), of course with a traditional examination and cross-examination carried out by the parties' advocates in front of the clerk.

161. Each party must at least consider the following points: (a) which elements in the case it is up to him to prove. The point is, as mentioned, that it will count against a party when the case is decided if the answer to a given point of fact is uncertain on the evidence; (b) how the party can attempt to remove this uncertainty, for example, through expert appraisal (survey, etc.); (c) what costs the party must expect to incur in this connection. Each party must pay the costs incurred by him in the process of litigation (*Rpl* section 311), but if he wins the case, he may have them fully or partially refunded by the other party (section 312, subsection 1 cf. our general cost principle in the administration of justice, the 'English rule').

Anything which is practicably possible to produce in court may be used in evidence, as the principle of free admissibility and assessment of evidence applies. Film, video, and tape recordings can thus also be used in evidence. If there is more than one possible way of proving a point, the best possible avenue should be selected. After the Court Reform 2007/2008, the procedure allows considerably broader scope for giving evidence, for example, by video, electronically recorded or transmitted directly during the trial.

162. An important role is played by the preparatory meeting according to *Rpl* section 353. For details about this preparatory meeting, *see* paragraph 139 above, where the agenda of this meeting, and the importance of it, are dealt with.

163. We have now reached the end of the pretrial proceedings. The court may decide when this stage is reached (cf. section 356, subsection 1, of the *Rpl*). This decision is not made arbitrarily or casually, but when the exchange of pleadings is completed, any expert appraisal performed, etc. If the court does not decide otherwise, the pretrial proceedings are ended on the day four weeks before the final oral hearing.

When the pretrial stage is complete, the court notes this on the case, and a barring of claims (negative prescription) now restricts the parties' scope for bringing new claims or new factual allegations (cf. section 358) on the principle of full and early notice. If a party wants to extend his claim or bring new arguments, he must first apply to the other party for an agreement to do so. If this application fails, he can ask the court, and the court must consider in its decision whether the delay was excusable.

If this is not the case, permission may still be granted if the other party has had an adequate opportunity to defend its interests (typically because there is still a long time before the date fixed for the trial), and/or if it would involve a disproportionate loss for the party wanting to bring new facts or arguments into the case if the request were denied. It is quite often the case that one of these criteria will result in permission, provided that the date for the trial is distant.

164. The date and time of the trial can be fixed (the case is 'set down for trial', *sagen berammes*). Either the date for the final oral hearing (*hovedforhandlingen*) is agreed upon by the court and the parties already at the preparation meeting according to section 353 or a separate notification of the date will be sent out, often after court staff have had phone contact with the parties or their lawyers. To assist the court and their own planning, the lawyers must always give an estimate of how long they think the oral hearing will take (half a day in court, one day, one and a half days, etc.). If this estimate is wrong, it is most inconvenient for the court and the parties themselves.

C. Judgment

165. Depending on the formulation of the claim, the plaintiff (or defendant submitting a counterclaim for independent trial) may aim to obtain a declaratory judgment (*anerkendelsesdom*) or an enforcement order (*fuldbyrdelsesdom*).

A declaratory judgment is not aimed at enforcement by the bailiff. Its point of issue may be whether the defendant must admit that he has acted wrongfully in relation to plaintiff by advertising in a certain way, that defendant must recognize the plaintiff's title to certain things, etc. Nevertheless, to the extent that a declaratory judgment grants plaintiff (now: judgment creditor) the title to some assets, the judgment may often be enforced indirectly because judgment creditor can use the judgment directly in enforcement proceedings as evidence of his title. The declaratory judgment may have established the requisite clarification for direct enforcement.

As implied by the term, the enforcement order is formulated with the intention that it should be enforced unless judgment debtor does not pay voluntarily before the date of enforcement (period of grace), which is normally fourteen days from the date of the judgment. Holding such a judgment in his hand, the judgment creditor can go to the bailiff's court after two weeks unless judgment debtor has appealed the judgment before then, and request that the judgment be enforced by levying execution against assets belonging to the judgment debtor.

A judgment can combine both declaration and enforcement. If the judgment both orders defendant to recognize that he has acted wrongfully, and orders him to pay certain specified costs, the cost element is enforceable. Similarly, a case may contain both declaratory claims such as questions regarding lawfulness, property rights, etc., and enforcement claims, for example, compensation for infringement of the law.

166. The vast majority of judgments handed down are declaratory (*konstaterende*), i.e., they declare what was – in principle – already valid law between the parties. However much a defendant may object to the notion that he should have to pay anything under the plaintiff's claim, the fact is that the claim does not *arise* from the judgment. It already *existed* from the date of origin (an infringement, an agreement). The judgment merely states its existence and size besides normally allocating costs.

The opposite of a declaratory judgment is a judgment which sets a precedent (*konstitutive*). Such judgments do not pronounce a state of law already existing (A owes DKK 10,000 to B) but set new precedents and obligations (A is divorced from B, this or that debt instrument is declared null and void, this or that decision made by a general assembly is set aside). This happens in that the judgment creates, changes, or abolishes a right. It is a characteristic feature of this type of judgment that its effect extends not only *inter partes* but also *erga omnes*, i.e., to all. A textbook example is judgments concerning civil status under family law. The same applies to declarations of death in cases of disappeared persons. Judgments awarding the title to property and cancellation judgments also set precedents.

Further explanatory examples include:

(1) Judgment in matrimonial proceedings. This is the decision which dissolves the marriage through divorce or separates the parties with certain associated consequences in law. The same applies to the court's decision in paternity and adoption cases.
(2) Judgments in cancellation cases. It is the judgment as such which orders the lost security to be null and void, i.e., cancels it.
(3) Judgment in a case on illegal decisions by a company's general meeting. It is the judgment which cancels the faulty decision of the meeting, or perhaps changes it if such is the claim before it.

167. City courts are allowed to prepare judgments which do not contain the complete case narrative (cf. section 218a, subsection 2 of the *Rpl*), provided that the case was heard by only one judge. Such a 'summary' city court judgment can, therefore, be limited to a brief summary of the parties' claims, provided that it gives a full account of the reasoning for its decision. The judgment must state that the case narrative is not complete. The judgment states the parties' claim/defence in a brief account of their arguments, the reasoning and the conclusion.

If such summary judgment is appealed, the court must issue a supplementary account of the case. The account must be submitted to the High Court as early as possible after the court has been advised that the case is appealed. A copy of the account is sent to each of the parties at the same time. The account must, in particular, contain an account of the evidence given by the parties and witnesses, whereas it is not normally necessary to include the content of documents in the case. As the main elements in the parties' closing statements are often apparent from arguments repeated in the judgment and from the reasoning, they will not normally be included in the account either. The account is prepared on the basis of the judge's personal notes.

Only a minority of all city court judgments are appealed. If the court feels certain that the judgment will be appealed, it is probably more practical to prepare the judgment in the traditional manner with a complete narrative.

168. Although a party may believe that the judge's account contains a mistake, the court cannot correct the account. This can only be done through appeal.[121] However, mere mistakes of writing, figures, etc., can be corrected without appeal, i.e., through a decision made by the court which has pronounced the judgment (*Rpl* section 221). *See,* for example, *UfR* 2000:1987 H on correction of the amount awarded through the judgment (from DKK 760,000 to 776,000). Larger 'mistakes' in the judgment cannot be corrected by the court itself, but can only be changed through appeal.

121. Cf. *UfR* 1997:1453 Ø, where one of the parties raised an objection to the account. The city court judge referred him to the High Court for clarification in the appeals case, and the High Court agreed. The judge could not make additions or corrections.

169. The grounds must be clearly stated in both judgments and interlocutory orders, i.e., they must be reasoned (cf. section 218, subsection 1, 1st sentence, of the *Rpl*). The account given in a civil judgment of the parties' oral arguments and comments during the case constitutes full evidence of it unless the contrary is proved (cf. section 218, subsection 4). The judgment is pronounced either in or without a court hearing, and if it is pronounced in a court hearing, the judgment must be read out (cf. section 219, subsection 3). The judgment must contain the parties' claims and a case narrative, including an account of the parties' arguments, as much of the evidence as is required, and a statement of the points of fact and law taken into consideration in the judgment, i.e., the reasoning (cf. section 218a).

170. Notwithstanding the individual style of judges and courts, a standard has developed over the decades regarding the structure of a judgment, the guidance it gives the parties in deciding an appeal, and its value as a precedent in other cases, as research material, etc.

In some countries, the conclusion is given first, followed by the grounds, but the Danish tradition dictates the following structure:

(1) introduction with a summary statement of the main issue of the case;
(2) the parties' claim/defence and main arguments;
(3) a detailed summary of the facts, i.e., the case narrative (*narratio*);
(4) evidence given by the parties and witnesses, any declarations, etc.;
(5) closing speeches;
(6) reasoning (grounds or premises, from *præmittere* = that which goes before) and findings;
(7) conclusion ('IT IS HELD THAT: ... ', '*THIKENDES FOR RET:* ... ').

171. When the trial is ended (and efforts to mediate in the first instance have failed to produce a settlement), the case is set down for judgment. This means that the *inter partes* stage is complete and that the case is now entirely in the hands of the court for deliberation and decision.

When the case is set down for judgment, the court must advise the date of judgment. As already mentioned, the court must, after the Court Reform 2007/2008, make its decision in civil cases 'with all due speed after the trial has ended', and when the case is set down for judgment or order, the court must indicate when the judgment or order will be given (cf. section 219, subsection 1, 1st sentence of the *Rpl*). City courts must hand down a judgment or order not later than four weeks after the case has been set down for judgment if the case is heard by a single professional judge. The time limit is two months in city court cases, with three judges, and in High Court cases.

These limits may, however, be extended in special cases (cf. section 219, subsection 2). In criminal cases, the judgment must be given 'with all due speed after the trial has ended', and the dominant principle is that if judgment cannot be given on the same day, it should follow within a week at the most, in trial by jury not later than the following day (cf. section 219a, subsection 1).

172. As already mentioned, as the main rule, everyone, without having to prove special interest in the case, has a right to obtain copies of judgments, however with prior anonymization in criminal judgments. There is no general access to all documents in civil or criminal cases, but some important documents are subject to public access. If in a civil case, the parties have summarized their claims and allegations before the oral hearing, such writs (called *sammenfattende processkrift* – summarizing writ, and *påstandsdokument* – summary of claims) are subject to public access.

II. Provisional Proceedings

A. *Cases on Private Law Matters*

173. The fact that legal proceedings are initiated does not automatically mean that all development of the matter comprised by the case is suspended. This principle applies to both civil law and public law cases.

The matter which forms the content of a civil law case can thus develop quite considerably while the case is pending. If, for example, the claim is that a particular action is wrongful, the claim itself does not prevent the defendant from continuing the action or whatever, while the case is pending. If the plaintiff wants to bar the defendant from acting in a particular manner before an enforceable judgment has been given in the case, he must apply for an *injunction* (*forbud eller påbud*, meaning that something is prohibited by court order) against defendant's action (cf. immediately below). If the plaintiff fears that the defendant will move his money to a haven from creditors or otherwise take steps to evade compliance with a (future, not yet rendered) judgment which may require him to pay a sum of money, the plaintiff must seek to have parts of defendant's assets *frozen* through seizure (*arrest*) (*see* immediately below).

With effect as from 1 July 2013, the Danish legislator has, upon advice from the Danish Civil Justice Council (*Retsplejerådet*, a permanent advisory organ which prepares amendments to Danish procedural law for comprehensive reforms to Danish civil proceedings), held that it is suitable to move the competence in injunction cases to the court which has to decide the main litigation, instead of obtaining an order from the bailiff's court, and then afterwards try both the substantive merits of the case and also the lawfulness of the interim measure before the ordinary court.

The outcome of these considerations is, as mentioned with effect from 1 July 2013, an extensive reformation of Danish interim measures, making any kind of interim measure possible (Danish: *forbud og påbud*, freely translated: ordering *not* to, or ordering *to*).

So, in IP cases concerning patents, trademarks, or copyright, one does not turn to the bailiff but to the court where the main case on the merits is to be instigated. Perhaps, at the same time, one also instigates the main case on the merits and also requests the court to take interim measures. Or perhaps, one instigates only the injunction case, and then, within a time limit of two weeks after having obtained a verdict in one's favour concerning the question of injunction, one will have to instigate a case on the merits – if such a case has not already been instigated through arbitration, through a Danish court case or through a foreign court case.

174. If a survey (*syn og skøn*) is a matter of urgency because an object is deteriorating rapidly or must be repaired soon to prevent further loss, the survey can be done before any proceedings are brought. This is called anticipatory taking of evidence (or: isolated taking of evidence, *isoleret bevisoptagelse*) (cf. section 343 of the *Rpl*), but the main rule is that the survey is done after the case is launched, i.e., in connection with the preparation of a civil case. Please note that such isolated taking of evidence has priority even to the venue provisions of the Brussels I Regulation. Thus, if a purchaser domiciled in Denmark has purchased goods from an Italian seller, and the goods seem to be faulty which is not recognized by the seller, the purchaser could, because the goods are located here in Denmark, turn to the local city court, and obtain an order for a survey in accordance with section 343 on isolated taking of evidence. The seller has better participate in this matter because the outcome will have a high degree of evidence attached to it, regardless of where the main proceedings on the merit of the case are to be conducted.

Section 343 on isolated taking of evidence can also be applied if the applicant is the victim of some offence, for example, where his copyright is being violated, but where he is not aware of who the offender is. In *TDC*, the Danish tele company was ordered to provide the necessary information in a case where the applicant's copyright to some computer games had been violated, and where he needed information from the tele company in order simply to locate and identify the offender.[122]

B. Cases on Public Law Matters

175. It follows from section 63, subsection 1 of the Constitution (*Grundloven*) with regard to public law that an administrative Act can be brought to court, but also that the obligation to comply with such Act is not stayed by the fact that legal proceedings are launched to test the validity of an administrative Act.

In *Gyproc A/S*, the Supreme Court thus had regard to the fact that the courts in principle possess the general authority to grant a stay of execution.[123] This concerned an obligation under competition law to report discount and bonus agreements. Section 63, subsection 1, 2nd sentence, of the Constitution thus merely states that the sheer launching of legal proceedings does not as such suspend plaintiff's duty of obedience, but the courts must use their scope for staying proceedings with caution, and only in clear cases. Although the Constitution does not prohibit a stay of execution, the clause must be allowed a certain restrictive effect, and although the existing rules do not exhaust the scope for the delay, they do indicate that the legislature is not unaware of this possibility.

The courts may decide any question concerning the limits of administrative powers (with the Constitution's rather old-fashioned but nevertheless valid words:

---

122. *UfR* 2003:2264 Ø.

123. *UfR* 1994:823 H, with comment by Supreme Court Judge Per Walsøe in *UfR* 1995 B, 128 et seq.

'*øvrighedsmyndighedens grænser*', the limits of administrative powers). No person wanting to raise such a question may, however, avoid temporary compliance with the authority's order by taking the question to the courts.

Individual statutes can, however, provide a stay of execution if legal proceedings are launched. With inspiration from EU law and other sources, the Supreme Court has also considered the fact that the Constitution does not preclude the courts from granting a stay of execution on the basis of a concrete evaluation, also in cases where this is not explicitly provided by law.

In his commentary, Walsøe refers to *Factortame I*.[124] It must presumably be concluded from this judgment that in cases where it is claimed that a national administrative decision is in contravention of EU law and where the national court has decided to submit the question to the European Court, the national court has the power under EU law to decide that proceedings pursuant to the decision must be stayed. There is harmony between this situation, Walsøe argues, and the situation where the Supreme Court confirms the existence of a general right also under Danish law to grant a stay of execution also outside those cases provided by law. However, Walsøe continues, there could be very little doubt that the launching of the case under discussion should not lead to a stay of execution. The Supreme Court deemed the effective enforcement of the statutory competition rules to be more important.

176. For the same general trend, *see Greenpeace*, where Greenpeace failed to gain support for its application for a stay in construction work in connection with proceedings against the Ministry of Transport, claiming that the Ministry was not legally entitled to let the construction of the Øresund Bridge go ahead.[125] The Supreme Court did not find that there were reasonable grounds for presuming that the Environmental Impact Assessment Directive's rules on the hearing which must precede construction work with environmental impact had been set aside, and there were, therefore, no grounds for granting a stay of execution.

In *Odense Staalskibsværft A/S*, the Supreme Court refused to grant a stay of execution, as the High Court had also refused.[126] The case concerned the question of whether a company must be registered under the rules on tax on waste and raw materials. The Supreme Court, which found no basis for an oral hearing of the appeal, observed that the damage which the company would suffer if it were later found that it had no duty of registration could not be deemed to be irreparable. Therefore, having regard for the fact that the Ministry of Taxation had a clear interest in having the registration performed without further delay, the court found that there were no 'special circumstances' which could justify a stay of execution on 'exceptional grounds'.

124. C-213/89.
125. *UfR* 1995:634 H.
126. *TfS* 1995:662 H.

C. Common Features in Provisional Proceedings

177. A common feature of the cases where (a) there is a basis for ordering an injunction or making a seizure under civil law, or (b) there is basis for decreeing a stay of execution on exceptional grounds in administrative law is that two fundamental conditions must be fulfilled:

(1) There must be a case of *fumus boni juris* (the smoke of sound law), i.e., it must be clear from a preliminary review of the case that a prima facie (at first sight) claim exists. (2) A case of *periculum in mora* (i.e., a danger in hesitating) must be proved, i.e., there must be a risk that the plaintiff will suffer irreparable harm if an injunction, etc., is not granted.

These principles are found in many countries in more or less identical form, and have been passed in EU law as a condition (A) allowing the ECJ to order injunctions or prescribe other interim measures in cases brought to the court: cf. Article 243 of the European Treaty, and (B) allowing national courts to, or prescribing that they must, prevent the enforcement of (B1) national rules presumed to contravene EU law (cf. *Factortame I*), or (B2) derived EU law presumed to contravene primary EU law or the basic rights and freedoms.

§2. Default Proceedings

178. If the defendant fails to appear, the result is not rejection of the case. Normally, the plaintiff will win the case, i.e., obtain judgment – by default – according to his claim. As noted, the defendant's failure to appear is not deemed to be an admission that the case against him is true. However, neither will he be given the same treatment as somebody who has contested the case against him.

A judgment by default against a defendant is based only on the writ and supporting documents, while in principle an acquittal can be based on everything. The court must also test all formal issues, for example, whether the writ was served, whether the notice to appear to the writ was observed, and whether the case is brought in the right court. The relatively modest testing performed by the court when a defendant fails to appear should be seen in light of the fact that the defendant has a broad scope for having the case resumed after the pronouncement of a default judgment (cf. section 367, compared with section 369, subsection 4).

179. A default judgment can be written in quite a simple fashion, simply by endorsing the writ, normally by attaching a stamp to it (cf. section 354, subsection 5). The appearance of such a judgment can become an interesting study object as it proceeds on its quest through the system: (1) the document first serves as a writ and is submitted to the court in this capacity; (2) it is then elevated to a default judgment in the case through the court's endorsement of the judgment ('*THI KENDES FOR RET:* … ', 'IT IS HELD THAT … '; (3) if judgment debtor fails to pay, judgment creditor endorses the judgment with a statement of his claim plus awarded costs, interest up to the date of the claim, court fee to the bailiff's court, etc., and sends the judgment with the statement and a request for execution to the bailiff's court (cf. below, paragraphs 267–271, on enforcement); (4) the bailiff's court where the judgment is presented endorses it with a statement on the presentation and what took place at the hearing in the bailiff's court, for example, that judgment debtor explained that he owned nothing against which execution could be levied, a so-called insolvency declaration.

180. Please note that many cases where a creditor would earlier go for a default judgment can now be treated according to the provisions of Demand for payment (*betalingspåkrav*) if the amount does not exceed DKK 100,000 (approximately EUR 13,300), cf. *Rpl* section 477a. The main conditions are as already mentioned that the claim does not exceed DKK 100,000 and that the debtor does not contest the claim. If the claim is contested, the creditor will have to take his case to court as in other civil proceedings, cf. section 477f.

181. A person against whom judgment has been given by default can request that the case be reopened within four weeks after the judgment was given. The court may reopen the case on exceptional grounds if the application is received later, but within one year after the judgment. The court can make it a condition for reopening the case that judgment debtor pays the costs awarded against him in the default judgment or provides security for payment. It is normally the defendant who can ask for a default judgment to be reconsidered, but cases do occur where a default judgment has been given against the plaintiff in relation to a counterclaim. In that case, it will, of course, be the plaintiff who applies for the case to be reopened. A case is reopened in the court which handed down the default judgment.

It is normally impossible to appeal a default judgment, as the person who defaulted can only appeal the case in the event of any procedural error in the handling of the case (cf. section 369, subsection 4). In such a situation, it is conceivable that a case could both be appealed (on the grounds of procedural error) and application made for its reopening. The reason why default judgments cannot normally be appealed is that an appeal would in effect make the appeals court perform a first instance hearing, and this would be inappropriate and contrary to the two-tier principle.

A request for a case to be reopened has in principle the same legal consequences as an appeal. The main consequence is that if a request for reopening is submitted before the expiry of the period of grace given in the judgment (normally fourteen days), the judgment will not be enforced by the bailiff's court. It should also be observed that the deadline for requesting a reopening is the same as the deadline for appeal from city court to the High Court.

§3. Ex Parte Proceedings

182. Ex parte proceedings, understood to mean one-sided actions where only one party is heard, are not a feature of Danish civil procedure, where the right of defence doctrine plays a highly essential role. Even summary forms of procedure, seizures and injunctions observe the right of defence, i.e., an adversarial principle.

Chapter 3. Review Proceedings

§1. Appeal

183. Appeals against judgments and interlocutory orders are means of legal remedy. A legal remedy is said to be ordinary if it can be applied within certain time limits without permission from any court or authority. Most remedies in Danish procedural law are by this definition ordinary.

The scope for correction of errors, etc., is, as already mentioned above under paragraph 168, very narrow (cf. section 221 of the *Rpl*). The court may, of its own accord or upon request, correct typing errors in words, names or figures, simple arithmetical errors and omissions relating only to the presentation. *See*, for example, *Hugo Nittebjerg* on correction of the amount awarded through the judgment (from DKK 760,000–776,000).[127] Larger 'mistakes' in the judgment cannot be corrected by the court itself but can only be changed through appeal.

184. By far the most common legal remedy is an appeal. When a case is appealed, it is taken to a court one level higher, where the appealed decision will be tested by a presumably more 'qualified' court. The appeal court's higher 'qualification' is apparent from the sheer fact that there will often be more judges on the bench than for a hearing in the lower court, but as the Court Reform 2007/2008 has introduced trial by panels of judges in the city courts (three professional judges, in some cases one or three professional judges plus two expert judges), this argument no longer holds entirely; indeed, one of the aims of the reform has been to provide more weight behind city court trials of complex cases, also in the hope of reducing the need for appeals. It is yet too early to conclude whether this goal has been fully obtained or not.

The fundamental principle applies that court decisions can be tried in two and only two instances (the two-tier principle), although in some cases permission may be granted for hearing in a third instance (and in some cases, permission must be granted even for hearing in two instances). Permission is obtained by application to the Appeals Permission Board (*Procesbevillingsnævnet*).

The appeal instances are as follows:

- City court judgments (*domme afsagt af en byret*) may be appealed to the High Court (except for the DKK 20,000 limit, cf. below).
- High Court judgments (*domme afsagt af Vestre Landsret eller Østre Landsret*) pronounced by High Court as the first instance (i.e., in cases referred from the city court to High Court because of the case's principal nature) may be freely appealed to the Supreme Court.
- High Court judgments pronounced by High Court as the second instance, that is judgments in cases which started in the city court, may only be appealed to the Supreme Court with appeal permission from the Appeals Permission Board (*Procesbevillingsnævnet*).

127. *UfR* 2000:1987 H.

- Judgments by the Maritime and Commercial Court (*Sø- og Handelsretten*) are now appealed to the Appeal Court (Western or Eastern Appeal Court, *Vestre Landsret* or *Østre Landsret*) where the case would have been dealt with if it had not been treated by the Maritime and Commercial Court. Some cases may be appealed directly to the Supreme Court. The case must be of principal character and must have general importance for the administration and development of law, or the case must have considerable impact for society, or 'other special reasons' must be in favour of the direct appeal to the Danish Supreme Court.

It is the court's decision which is appealed. The decision is normally clear from the conclusion to the judgment ('*THI KENDES FOR RET:* ... ', 'IT IS HELD THAT: ... ').

If it should occur that the decision is found only in the reasoning section of the judgment, it may still be appealed: cf. *Bingo Foto A/S*, where, however, the court found that the reasoning contained no decision.[128]

185. An appeal may concern decisions (rulings and orders, in Danish: *kæremål* or simply: *kære*) made in the course of the case (cf. section 389). However, after judgment has been pronounced in the case, separate appeal of rulings and other decisions cannot take place (section 390). The difference between the appeal of a judgment (Danish: anke) and appeal of rulings and other decisions (*kære*) is that the former results in a final oral hearing in the appeal court, whereas the latter is as a main rule treated only on written basis.

186. Judgments rejecting the case, for example, because it has not been brought to the right court, can only be taken to one level higher court by *kære* (cf. section 369, subsection 3), i.e., on a written basis. This is the situation if, for example, the court has found that there is no venue in Denmark for the case. If the court finds that another Danish court is competent, it refers the case to that court. If the case is rejected for other reasons, for example, because the court finds that arbitral proceedings have been agreed by the parties, and that consequently, the courts lack competence in the matter, the judgment that rejects the case must be brought to the higher instance through ordinary appeal, i.e., with a final oral hearing in the appeal court.

Certain parts of a judgment can be appealed separately. This applies to decisions on costs and procedural sanctions: cf. section 369, subsection 2, cf. for example, *MG Biler I/S*,[129] but with regard to costs, only subject to the appeals threshold amount of DKK 20,000, approximately EUR 2,600 (cf. section 391, subsection 1). However, if no costs are awarded, no permission to appeal is required, subject to motives and court practice (cf. *B6 af 1972 A/S*).[130]

The scope for appealing interlocutory orders to the Supreme Court is particularly narrow (cf. section 392). Orders and rulings given by the High Court acting as CFI under section 253 (i.e., when the court has decided separately on one out of several

128. *UfR* 1981:264 H.
129. *UfR* 1999:1398 H.
130. *UfR* 1999:1635 V.

issues in the case) can only be appealed to the Supreme Court with the latter Court's permission (cf. subsection 1). Other decisions can only be appealed to the Supreme Court with the permission of the Board of Appeals Permission (cf. subsection 2).

187. An appeals limit of DKK 20,000, approximately EUR 2,600, was introduced in 1990 (and the amount was increased from DKK 10,000 to DKK 20,000 in 2014), requiring permission to appeal cases falling below the limit value. This limit applies to:

- the appeal of city court judgments in civil law cases (cf. section 368, subsection 1);
- the appeal of city court interlocutory orders and decisions on costs (cf. section 389, subsection 2);
- the appeal of decisions in city court judgments on costs (cf. section 391, subsection 1);
- decisions by the bailiff's court on execution and costs (cf. section 584).

Petition for appeal to the second instance must be submitted to the Appeals Permission Board (*Procesbevillingsnævnet*). The criteria for being granted the right of appeal to the second instance are that it is a case of 'general public importance' or that other 'special reasons' apply. The purpose of introducing the limit of DKK 20,000 was to save resources, but the resources spent on handling the applications are at least as great as the resources it would have taken to try the cases on their merits in the High Court.

188. Judgments given by a High Court acting as Court of Appeal cannot be appealed to the Supreme Court without permission for the third instance hearing from the Appeals Permission Board, *Procesbevillingsnævnet* (cf. section 371, subsection 1 of the *Rpl*). This also applies to cases which have only been tested in one court.[131]

It used to be the case that in order to be granted permission to appeal to the court of the third instance, the case had to be either of general public importance, i.e., a matter of principle was involved, or of major importance to the plaintiff (or estimated to be of major importance to plaintiff). The only principle now applying is that of public (principal) importance.

The 'mere' question of a wrong decision is not enough to warrant an appeal to the third instance. Every legal system must accept a certain level of risk of 'wrong' decisions – just like (without comparison whatsoever) it has been said about the US Supreme Court that the court 'is not there to right a wrong'. If a two-tier system is to have any meaning, the criterion by which third-tier appeals are granted must be narrow.

This is not, of course, to say that the board may not be influenced in its decision by a belief that the High Court decision was wrong. In a small number of cases, the right of appeal to the third instance would seem fully justified simply based on a

131. Cf. *UfR* 1999:1776 H, on a civil law compensation claim (ancillary claim during a criminal case), which was not tested by the city court, but which the High Court tested on its merits.

wrong decision. This applies where costs have been awarded against the 'wrong' party or have clearly been 'wrongly' calculated (and correction through section 221 is impossible because it is not just an error of writing).

189. Some categories of cases which the board has found of general public importance are mainly cases concerning the interpretation of the law, cases challenging fundamental principles developed in case law and/or established through legal theory, cases where it appears that there is a need for establishing new case law or to clarify whether the existing state of law ought to be changed, or where a previous decision by the Supreme Court, possibly a dissenting judgment, must be deemed doubtful. The fact that the city court and the High Court have reached different results, or that the High Court's decision was given with a dissenting judgment, does not, on the other hand, constitute general public importance.

If it is claimed that the case has major importance for a series of similar cases, intervention (and hence argumentation) from a trade association, interest organization or similar with the board can serve to strengthen the board's perception that the case is a matter of general importance. It may therefore not be deduced from section 27 of the *Rpl*, under which a public authority which has intervened in the proceedings pursuant to section 252, subsection 2 may support the party's request to the board with a written declaration that 'support declarations' from bodies other than public authorities may not accompany applications to the boards; they certainly can.

190. As a main rule, the parties cannot waive their right to appeal before the judgment has been given in the case in question (cf. section 370). However, one of the items of the Court Reform 2007/2008 was to introduce, in cases between business undertakings, that they can already before litigation has been instigated, i.e., already in their contract, agree that they waive their right of appeal. Such waiver may be conditional, for example, conditional upon a three-judge bench, thereby approaching the composition of the court somewhat to what is when in arbitral proceedings, which is exactly the idea with this special possibility of waiver.

In all kinds of cases, subsequent waiver of the right to appeal plays an important practical role. Before the Court Reform 2007/2008, a waiver could be given tacitly, for example, through the voluntary satisfaction of the judgment without simultaneously reserving the right to appeal: cf. *UfR* 1990:624 H, where the judgment debt had been paid 'in full and final settlement'. However, the reform introduced a provision according to which a waiver must be explicit (*Rpl* section 370, subsection 5). Thus, case law older than the reform has on this area lost its significance.

191. The deadline for appeal is four weeks. This applies to appeal both from city court to the High Court and from the High Court to the Supreme Court (cf. section 372, subsection 1). The period runs from the date of the judgment (cf. section 372, subsection 1, *in fine*).

Notice of appeal must be in the hands of the appeal court before the expiry of the deadline: cf. *UfR* 1991:74 Ø, where the notice was sent to the court the day before the expiry of the limit but was only received six days after expiry because of a mail strike, and where the appeal was rejected. However, please note that in small claims cases, the notice of appeal must be submitted to the city court itself (cf. section 410, subsection 2, of the *Rpl*), and consequently an appeal which took place in due time, but to the Court of Appeal instead of the city court, was rejected in *UfR* 2010:21 Ø.

If the deadline for appeal is exceeded, the appeal court can allow the appeal to go ahead until one year after the date of the judgment on exceptional grounds (cf. section 372, subsection 2 of the *Rpl*).

192. A case is appealed by handing in a notice of appeal (*ankestævning*) to the appeal court's office (cf. section 372, subsection 2 of the *Rpl*).

Since 2018, when all of the Danish courts were digitalized, the appeal is considered to have taken place when the appellant has clicked 'Acknowledge' (*godkend*) in accordance with his or her appeal in the digitalized Case Portal. An appeals notice must contain the following (cf. sections 373–374): (1) indication of which judgment is appealed; (2) indication of the defendant's address; (3) appellant's claim; (4) arguments, documents and other evidence on which appellant intends to rely and which were not invoked in the earlier instance (so-called *nova*); (5) indication of a postal address in Denmark where communications in the case may be sent to the appellant and where any documents may be served.

The judgment to be appealed must be appended to the notice with copies of the writ and the documents to be relied upon.

The appeal court arranges to have the notice served on the respondent (without cost) (cf. section 375).

Appellant can claim that the decision of the lower instance should be either: (a) changed, (b) overturned or (c) remitted for renewed trial in the lower court (cf. section 369, subsection 1). It is important to notice that appeal courts in Denmark, including the Supreme Court, do not merely function as cassation courts, *cours de cassation*, which can sustain or uphold the judgment from the lower instance. On the contrary, the appeal court can try the merits of the case in full.

However, the appeal may not claim affirmation, not even with reservation for a change (increase) in the claim or the performance of an expert appraisal (cf. *Ole Hougaard*).[132]

193. The appeal court sets a date by which the respondent must submit his writ of defence. However, the respondent does not have to submit any writ of defence if he merely wants the judgment from the lower instance upheld, without wishing to bring any kind of new allegations, evidence or other nova into the appeal case (*Rpl* section 377). Respondent does not have to submit a writ of defence, and if he does not submit such a writ, he is deemed to argue for having the judgment of the lower court upheld.

A respondent's writ of defence – if any – must contain the following (cf. section 376): (1) respondent's claim; (2) indication of appellant's claim, arguments, documents and other evidence on which a respondent intends to rely and did not rely on in the earlier instance; (3) indication of a postal address in Denmark where communications in the case may be sent to the respondent, and where any documents may be served. Copies of the documents invoked must be appended to the Notice.

132. *UfR* 1991:59 V.

Objections to the appeal on points of law, for example, that the period allowed for appeal has expired, are forfeited unless made in the writ of defence (cf. sections 376, subsection 2, and 382, subsection 2). This does not mean, however, that the appeal court itself should be excluded from – ex officio – regarding the appeal as having taken place too late (*Rpl* section 337); the appeal court can at any time raise the question of whether the appeal has taken place after the deadline, and thus should be rejected by the appeal court.

194. The appeals court can allow further exchange of pleadings, and a full pre-trial may be held (cf. section 378).

195. Appeals are in principle heard orally. The appeals court may, however, prescribe a written hearing (cf. section 387), and this occurs particularly in the Supreme Court.

Currently, the proportion of civil law cases before the Supreme Court which are heard in writing has grown to more than one-third. This increases the court's capacity considerably. If an appeals case which should be heard orally lapses at a late date because the appeal is cancelled, the judges' capacity may be utilized by the court distributing the files in a civil law case which is to be heard in writing, and which the judges may then deliberate on the vacant day.

An appeal hearing generally proceeds in the same manner as a first instance hearing, with a complete retrial (full appeal) – with the important exception, however, that a full hearing has already taken place and is reflected in the judgment from the lower instance. The parties often agree that it is unnecessary to repeat all the hearing of evidence from the lower court, and merely produce documentation to the appeals court of the evidence given in the lower court.

196. A very important question in practical terms is whether the subject matter of the case may be changed in the course of the appeal trial through the production of fresh claims, allegations (arguments) and/or evidence (*nova*). A distinction is here made between *nova* concerning the original subject matter (cf. sections 380–383) and *nova* concerning a new subject matter (cf. section 384). It is more problematic to allow *nova* concerning a new subject matter, and the two-tier system can be undermined by its production.

New documents and other evidence may be freely produced, provided the court and the other party are informed of this at the latest two weeks before the hearing. However, the court can always allow the evidence if the failure to produce it in time is deemed to be excusable.

New claims and new facts can be produced with the permission of the other party or the court. The court will normally allow new material to be produced if the court finds it excusable that it was not produced earlier or if there is a reason to presume that a refusal will involve a disproportionate loss for the party in question. For an appeal to the High Court (but not to the Supreme Court), permission may also be granted if the other party has adequate opportunity to defend his own interests. The new claims and arguments must normally be produced in the pretrial stage of the appeal: cf. section 382 (the principle of full and early notice in appeals cases).

If the new materials concern a new subject matter, the court's permission is always required. It is not enough to obtain the other party's permission (cf. section 384).

197. If a respondent fails to appear, the case proceeds, and the appeals court makes its decision on the basis of the material before it and the appellant's evidence and oral statements. If the respondent fails to appear for the pretrial, the court can allow the case to proceed upon the appellant's request on the basis of the written materials before it and a brief from the appellant. Respondent won the case in the first instance, and his absence may indicate that he feels certain that the lower court made the right decision.

If both parties fail to appear, the court cancels the appeal.

198. The appeal court's judgment will typically uphold or change the appealed judgment. It is also conceivable that the appeal will be turned down, for example, because the period of appeal has expired or it is found that the appellant has waived his right to appeal.

§2. Cassation

199. The appeal court's decision may reverse the lower court's decision (*ophævelse*). A reversal will always be combined with something else: It may be: (1) remission to a lower court; (2) denial of the case because it does not belong in the courts; (3) referral of the case to the right court; or (4) remission to an administrative authority, for example, a tax authority.

The case is typically remitted to the lower court if this court has committed a serious procedural error. In case of minor procedural errors which are not judged to have influenced the lower court's decision, the appeal court merely draws attention to the error. The case will also be remitted to the lower court if it has wrongly rejected the case, for example, if the lower court found that there is no venue in Denmark for the case, but the appeal court found Danish courts competent in the matter.

200. Apart from the above cases, where the appeal court functions merely as a kind of 'cassation court', the Danish appeals bodies in Danish civil procedure are not limited to cassation which merely affirms or reverses the appealed judgment. As is clear from the previous comments, the Court of Appeal undertakes a full hearing of the case, subject only to the proviso previously explained regarding fresh evidence, a condition aimed at ensuring that the case preserves its 'identity' in the appeal. It is important that there be scope for bringing new evidence in the appeals court. Despite the requirement regarding 'identity', a case may, therefore, present a very different aspect during appeal than it did in the lower court.

§3. Extraordinary Appeals

201. Under section 399 of the *Rpl*, the Supreme Court can allow extraordinary appeals of Supreme Court decisions, which of course cannot normally be appealed. The conditions for extraordinary appeals are so strict that several years normally pass between approvals of applications for an extraordinary appeal.

An extraordinary appeal may also be granted with regard to High Court judgments (cf. section 399, subsection 2). This avenue for obtaining Supreme Court permission to launch an extraordinary appeal or, in other words, the right to appeal to the third instance granted directly by the Supreme Court is secondary to the same right granted by the Appeals Permission Board: cf. *Britta Lunde*.[133]

133. *UfR* 1999:1377 H.

Part V. Incidents

202. A distinction must be made between the formal and the substantive aspects of a case.

The formal aspect concerns the issue of whether the case can be tried at all by the court in question, or whether it must be denied or referred to another court. This aspect is often referred to as grounds for dismissal. Questions regarding how the case should be heard, including whether expert opinions should be solicited, evidence taken, etc., are also aspects of the procedure.

The substantive aspect, or the merits of the case, concerns the testing of the claims, apart from claims regarding dismissal or referral raised during the case. The merits of the case are thus the question of whether and to what extent judgment should be handed down against the defendant or whether he should be acquitted.

The formal aspect is generally decided with reference to procedural rules, while the merits of the case are generally decided on the basis of the substantive rules of law applying to its subject matter.

As a main rule, the court must consider and decide any formal issue of its own accord, whereas it only considers the merits of the case upon application from the parties. These main rules are, however, certainly not without exceptions.

An example of where formal issues are dependent on the parties' own position is the question of venue: A tacit agreement will be presumed to have been entered into if the defendant, including consumer defendants, appears in court (or submits a defence in the case of a court where the pretrial stage is conducted in writing with no oral hearings) without objecting to the court's jurisdiction (cf. section 248, subsection 1, 2nd sentence). If, on the other hand, the defendant does not attend at all, the court must initiate a check to see if the case has been brought to the right court.

An example where merits of the case are considered by the court without application by the parties is the question of legal costs. Here, the court on its own initiative makes a decision concerning the costs (although of course the court is ready to hear the arguments of the parties, often in the last part of their oral observations during the final hearing).

203. The question of whether time limits have been observed and whether the subject matter of the case is governed by an arbitration clause are formal aspects. However, the question of who is rightly the plaintiff or the defendant is part of the substance of the case.

The defendant may have objections regarding points of both law and fact, although most objections concern facts. Regarding the facts, the defendant may claim acquittal, arguing that he does not owe plaintiff anything, and with regard to the law, he may claim dismissal, arguing that the case cannot be heard in a Danish court. A position of this kind would be reflected in a primary claim for dismissal and a secondary claim for acquittal (the claims of defendant are formulated as follows: *Principal påstand: afvisning. Subsidiær påstand: frifindelse*).

If the court supports the defendant's claim for dismissal, there is no need for him to spend time and money launching a defence with regard to the facts of the case. He can limit his statement of defence to his claim for dismissal and ask that it be heard and decided first (cf. section 351, subsection 4, cf. also section 253 of the *Rpl*).

This position would be reflected in a claim for dismissal followed by a request that this claim be tested separately, and the comment that the right to objection on points of merits of the case is thereby reserved. If the court upholds the claim for dismissal, the claim for acquittal is superfluous. If it is not upheld, the case must proceed to be heard on its merits. Pleading is then resumed, and in his next pleadings, i.e., the defence proper, the defendant must submit his claim with regard to the facts of the case, for example, acquittal, and his arguments in support of his claim.

204. When an objection regarding a point of law, for example, a claim for dismissal, has been made, the court sets down the case for a hearing on a point of procedure (so-called *formalitetsprocedure*, i.e., separate claims, allegations and decision on the formality), at which the parties present arguments in support of their claims. Plaintiff will argue that the case should be admitted, i.e., he argues that the court should proceed to a full trial of the case, while the defendant will argue that the case should be dismissed. If the court admits the case for full trial despite a claim for its dismissal, it does so in a ruling. If it dismisses the case, it is done by an order for dismissal.

205. An order for dismissal may be appealed pursuant to the rules on appeal of interlocutory orders (cf. section 391, subsection 3), and not under the rules applying to appeals against judgments, despite the fact that an order for dismissal constitutes a final judgment (at this court). If the order for dismissal is given by the High Court acting as a court of the second instance, an appeal will require permission from the Appeals Permission Board (*Procesbevillingsnævnet*).

If, however, a ruling has been given to the effect that the case will be admitted for trial on its merits, such a ruling can normally not be appealed independently to a higher court. It is then generally necessary to wait until judgment has been given in the case and include this objection when appealing the judgment (cf. section 253, subsection 4). Since the law was changed in 1998, the questions of law here discussed have come under the category of interlocutory decrees in section 253, which also include decisions on valid law, jurisdiction, competence of the court, statutory limits, the capacity to sue, and lapse and failure to act.

206. Decision pronounced according to section 253 (*delafgørelser*, part decisions) are res judicata, also for the court itself, and they cannot be changed by the court itself, cf. *UfR* 2008:1707 V on a decision whether general conditions for Danish forwarders had been agreed upon by the parties or not.

207. If a decision on a point of law is made during an appeal against a judgment or an interlocutory order, it follows automatically from the two-tier principle that it cannot be freely appealed but will require permission by the Appeals Permission Board: cf. section 371 of the *Rpl* on appeals against judgments and section 392 on appeals against interlocutory orders.

Part VI. Legal Aid and Legal Costs

Chapter 1. Legal Aid

208. A party: (1) who has reasonable grounds for taking legal action; (2) whose income is below a certain limit; (3) who does not have a private legal aid insurance covering legal aid in this matter, can be granted legal aid by application (cf. section 325 of the *Rpl*). Please note that the legal aid provisions are now secondary to private insurance: First, it must be examined to what extent the insurance covers and legal aid from the state must be regarded as a secondary source of help after the insurance. One might speak of a partly 'privatization' of legal aid. However, the interaction between public legal aid and private legal insurance seems to function well in practice.

The income limits for public-private aid are adjusted annually in a Ministry of Justice proclamation. The limits for 2022 are as follows: A yearly income up to DKK 348,000 (approximately EUR 46,400), for persons living with a spouse or a cohabitant: DKK 442,000 (approximately EUR 58,900). If the application concerns a matrimonial case, i.e., spouse against spouse, of course only each person's own income is taken into consideration, not the whole 'family's' income.

The application for public legal aid must be submitted to the Department of Civil Affairs (*Civilstyrelsen*), which is a part of the Ministry of Justice. If legal aid is denied, the case can be appealed to the Appeals Permission Board (*Procesbevillingsnævnet*), which has already been mentioned several times in connection with the competence of appeal permission, but which also possesses the competence as instance of recourse in legal aid matters (the board is run in two separate divisions, one concentrated on appeal permission and one concentrated in recourse in legal aid matters). But as mentioned: first, the applicant must turn to his private insurance for legal aid under the insurance.

Both plaintiff and defendant can obtain legal aid. It may therefore well happen that both parties to a case have received legal aid.

Only as a rare exception, legal aid is granted in cases concerning: (1) libel action; or (2) a party's independent commercial enterprise (*Rpl* section 328, subsection 4). If, however, the case involves a small firm and the case is vital for the owner's financial survival, legal aid cannot be entirely ruled out in a commercial case.

If the party who has been granted legal aid dies, the grant is now automatically terminated, but it will then pass to the person(s) with a legal interest in the continuation of the case, typically the deceased estate: cf. section 331, subsection 5 of the *Rpl*.

If the plaintiff is granted legal aid, no court fee is paid on the writ (cf. section 331). A person receiving legal aid is assigned a lawyer by the court. This is normally the lawyer who examined the case for the person and applied for legal aid on his behalf. The lawyer's fee and any costs are paid by the public purse. If an expert opinion (survey) must be obtained on behalf of the party who has received legal aid, this too is paid by the public purse.

209. If the party in possession of free legal aid loses the case, the costs awarded to the other party are also paid by the public purse (cf. section 331, subsection 1, no. 4). If the other party loses the case, he must pay costs to the public purse as if there were no legal aid (cf. section 332). Otherwise, it would be the other party who reaped the benefit from the granting of legal aid. The other party must also pay a fixed amount assessed to equal the court costs which would have been payable in the absence of legal aid.

It is the Department of Civil Affairs (*Civilstyrelsen*, under the Ministry of Justice) which decides (with right of appeal to the Appeals Permission Board, *Procesbevillingsnævnet*) whether reasonable grounds exist for taking legal action, i.e., whether it would be reasonable to have the case tested in court. The case need not be a definite winner. The important question is whether it could reasonably be taken to court (cf. immediately below for the overall assessment of this question).

In some cases there are by definition reasonable grounds for going to court, including situations where a consumer has had his case tested by the relevant complaints board (e.g., the Consumer Complaints Board, *Forbrugerklagenævnet*, or the Danish Complaint Board of Banking Services, *Det finansirlle ankenævn*) and won the case, but the other party (the seller, the bank, etc.) either refuses to comply with the board's decision or demands that it be tested in court (cf. section 335a). The Ombudsman (*Folketingets Ombudsmand*, or simply: *Ombudsmanden*) can recommend that legal aid be granted in a case under his auspices (cf. section 23 of the Act on the Ombudsman).

Even if the party in possession of free legal aid wins the case, he might in some cases be ordered to compensate the public purse for its expenses in the case (*Rpl* section 332, subsection 2). This provision may especially be applied if the winning party with free legal aid has gained so much through the litigation that it would seem unfair to let the taxpayers carry the burden of the case. Cf., for example, *UfR* 2009:277 V where the winning party in a matrimonial case was awarded DKK 550,000 from his ex-spouse, and the court found that it was fair to let himself carry the salaries of approximately DKK 28,000 for his own counsel.

210. As noted, the lawyer assigned to a free legal aid party receives his fee plus VAT from the public purse (cf. section 334). The fee is fixed by an independent decision by the court which assigned the lawyer. The lawyer may not accept any additional fee from the client to whom he has been assigned (cf. section 334, subsection 5).

211. What generally happens is that the party goes to a lawyer, who then submits the application for legal aid on his behalf. If the party receiving legal aid has no contact with a lawyer who will accept assignment to his case, the court assigns one of the lawyers permanently appointed by the Ministry of Justice (against payment on a case basis) to conduct legal proceedings for parties receiving legal aid within that jurisdiction (cf. section 334). These so-called court-assigned counsels are also bound to provide free legal advice to people contacting them who fulfil the financial conditions for obtaining legal aid (cf. next paragraph). They also have a duty to assist in the preparation of applications for free legal aid. All the lawyer's costs arising from the submission of the application for free legal aid are paid by the public purse.

212. Legal aid also includes enforcement of a judgment (cf. section 331, subsection 3, of the *Rpl*). If the party receiving free legal aid has been awarded a sum by the court and if judgment debtor does not comply with the judgment, judgment creditor will automatically receive free legal aid for the case in the bailiff's court, so that no court fee is payable, and the public purse pays the lawyer.

213. If legal proceedings are launched, the court must be advised to what extent the costs will be covered by legal aid insurance, as it is only the remainder that must be covered by any legal aid grant from the public. The insurance has a maximum sum for each insured event.

The insurance company is not a party to the case, and the court's decision on costs cannot, therefore, involve the insurance company (cf. *Tryg Forsikring*),[134] but as the company will nevertheless end up holding the bill within the limits of the insurance agreement, the company has the same right to appeal the decision on costs as the parties.[135]

214. Legal aid is divided into three steps (*Rpl* section 323), where step 1 is paid 100% by the public, step 2 is paid 75% by the public and step 3 is paid 50% by the public. Step 1 is for basic help on a purely oral basis, whereas step 2 is more extended advice and step 3 is for specific advice in obtaining conciliation in an already pending dispute. Step 1 is for everyone, regardless of income, whereas step 2 and 3 is dependent on income.

Typical legal aid problems concern family, inheritance, purchase and tenancy law. Legal aid is not available to persons publicly charged with or accused of a criminal offence or to business people in cases of a predominantly business nature.

Legal aid includes advice and the drawing up of a small number of written documents of the usual kind, including the application for free legal aid, pleadings in court cases, the preparation of estate division agreements, uncomplicated testaments and marriage settlements, and also participating in meetings and hearings.

215. Many cities have a legal aid service; major cities often have more than one. This is a kind of roster system, typically organized by the local lawyers' association, offering free, anonymous, and verbal advice. In principle, everybody has

134. *UfR* 1990:807 Ø.
135. *UfR* 1990:885 H.

access to this service irrespective of their personal income. If it is found that the client requires further assistance, he or she will typically be referred to a lawyer, with or without legal aid.

There are also private legal aid services. They are typically organized by student unions, trade unions or tenants' associations. Relative to the public legal aid service, private legal aid services undertake more casework proper. Such private legal aid is mostly free and may be financed indirectly through the membership fee.

Both public and private legal aid services receive financial support from the Ministry of Justice.

Chapter 2. Legal Costs

216. One of the most important points to be considered prior to any decision to take legal action is the costs associated with such action. The court will not consider the allocation of costs until final judgment is given in the case, but the parties must necessarily consider this aspect much earlier.

Every court case is associated with a risk that the case is not what it appears in terms of evidence and/or law, and that it may be lost wholly or in part (i.e., the risk of going to court). The price of this risk must be calculated before a writ is taken out or the case abandoned.

217. The Danish cost system is, similar to the system in many other countries, based on three important principles:

(1) Any person initiating legal proceedings (e.g., by submitting a writ, appointing a lawyer, etc.) carries the initial responsibility for the costs involved: cf. section 311, subsection 1, 1st sentence, of the *Rpl.*
(2) If, upon request by one of the parties, the court approves the taking of a particular procedural measure (e.g., appointing a surveyor), the court can decide that the other party must, until further decision at the end of the case, carry the costs if it is in his interest that the step is taken, or the court can decide that the costs should be divided in a particular manner (cf. section 311, subsection 2).
(3) The losing party is normally ordered to pay costs to the winning party (cf. section 312, subsection 1). This principle under which the loser pays the costs of the case is found in most other countries as well (the US being a notable exception). The principle is known as the *English rule*. Legal costs comprise: (i) court fees; (ii) such expenses in obtaining expert opinions (surveys) as the other party may have paid; (iii) an *estimated* sum to cover the winning party's legal costs (cf. section 316). Court fees, survey expenses, etc., are paid in full, whereas legal costs are only paid with a 'suitable amount' (section 316).

Some countries, including Sweden, not only award an estimated sum but also refund all the winner's (relevant) costs upon presentation of invoice; i.e., they award costs 'in full'.

When the amount paid in costs is estimated, as the Danish system is, there is a risk of incurring a 'loss' in taking legal action as the actual costs payable in legal fees, etc., may exceed the amount awarded in costs. Thus, the winner will now and then experience that in spite of having won the case, and in spite of having his expenses repaid by the loser, it still represented a 'loss' for him to litigate in the matter.

Sometimes, one might feel that courts are perhaps a little too reluctant in awarding the winner a refund of his reasonable costs. *See*, e.g., *Nomeco A/S* where an injunction had been filed, but dismissed, against the defendant's marketing of a medicine which the plaintiff felt was contrary to his patent rights. The defendant demanded a refund of his expert expenses during the injunction case and was awarded a refund of his expense amounting to DKK 145,000 for an expert opinion from a professor in pharmacology, but not any part of his expense amounting to DKK 1,400,000 for expert assistance concerning patent law. The defendant's total expenses for his defence – successfully – during the injunction amounted to DKK 2,800,000.[136]

To 'defend' this system, two items are to be mentioned: First, the alternative: to refund the winner's costs in full would make the litigation risk even larger than today for both parties and would increase the burden on the looser. Second, the Court Reform 2007/2008 was indeed aware of the possibility that the winner after all 'lost' money on his case – and the response to this problem was to adjust the legal costs (counsel fees) which are calculated into the decisions of courts when awarding costs to the winner. These fees were adjusted upwards, in order for them to correspond approximately to the fees that would normally (as a 'standard' be invoiced by lawyers in the cases concerned).

218. The presidents of the Western and the Eastern High Courts have issued a common set of Tariffs, and guidance can be sought in these Tariffs, but deviation from the Tariffs may very well be justified in individual cases. The full Tariffs can be found on the webpage of The Danish Bar and Law Society (*Advokatsamfundet*): http://www.advokatsamfundet.dk. Only some examples from the Tariffs: If the value of the case is between DKK 58,001 and DKK 230,000, a 'normal' fee would be between DKK 13,000 and DKK 43,000 + VAT. Value DKK 575,001–1,150.000: fee DKK 43,000–95,000 + VAT. Value DKK 2,300,001–5,750,000: fee DKK 101,000 –259,000 + VAT. Over DKK 5,750,000: an estimate according to the specific circumstances, with 3% of the case value as the main rule. Please note that the DKK equals approximately EUR 0.13; to get from DKK to EUR, please divide by a factor of 7.5.

Please observe that these Tariffs do *not* impose binding restrictions on practising lawyers. What they charge their client is a matter of agreement between lawyer and client, however always subject to a fairness test. The client can bring this matter before the Disciplinary Board of the Danish Bar and Law Society (*Advokatnævnet*) in Copenhagen. Disputes on lawyer's fees can also be taken to court. The Disciplinary Board also hears and decides complaints over an advocate's professional conduct. However, claims for damage must be decided by the courts.

The Tariffs merely indicate what is, as a good average and standard, recognized by the courts as a fair and usual legal expense for the winner's own legal fees. However, lawyers will certainly have a look at the Tariffs before charging their client, and if the actual invoice deviates too much from the Tariffs, the lawyer owes his client a good explanation.

The 'standard' fee for court mediation (*retsmægling*) conducted by one of the authorized mediators attached to the courts, often local practising lawyers, would be DKK 8,740 + VAT. If the mediation lasts more than approximately five hours, the fee will be increased by DKK 1,790 + VAT per additional hour.

219. If both parties win and lose approximately the same in the litigation, there is no 'winner' and no 'loser'. Before the Court Reform 2007/2008, the court would

136. *UfR* 2009:762 H.

in such cases let each party carry his own costs, but after the reform, the view on such an outcome has changed somewhat. It is often rather a matter of coincidence who instigated the litigation, and who consequently paid the court fee, and by sticking to the old practice one actually lets that party carry the court fee, although he is just as much winner as loser of the case. With *Malernes Fagforening Jylland Syd*, this practice was abandoned in favour of a new practice which more consequently and precisely divides the total costs, including the court fee, equally between the parties.[137]

220. If the winning party is VAT-registered, he will be awarded his legal costs *less* VAT, as the VAT will be refunded via his VAT account. If, on the other hand, the winning party is not VAT-registered, or if the case does not concern his VAT-registered business, he will receive costs *plus* VAT (again: at an estimated amount with a solid starting point in the Tariffs). The losing party receives no deduction for the amount payable in VAT (simply because the VAT is not deductible for him on his VAT accounts), and the VAT amount must *not*, therefore, be listed separately in the decision on costs.

Every writ and every defence document should, therefore, state whether the case concerns or does not concern the relevant party's VAT-registered company so that the court is aware of whether the party should be awarded costs with or without VAT if he wins the case.

221. The dominant principle is that only the losing party, not his lawyer, is ordered to pay costs to the other party. In quite exceptional cases, however, a lawyer may also be made liable for costs in, *for example,* unnecessary protraction of the case (cf. section 319 of the *Rpl*), or failure to perform his duty, for example, by having advised his client to undertake, and having conducted, a clearly groundless case. *See*, e.g., *UfR* 1999:99 H, in which a lawyer was ordered to share his clients' (some limited partners') costs in connection with a groundless case brought against a bank. The bank's lawyer had repeatedly advised the plaintiffs' lawyer that the claim against the bank had no basis in fact.

222. When a writ is submitted to the court, the court fee (*retsafgift*) calculated according to the rules of the Court Fees Act (*retsafgiftsloven*) must be attached. The court fees have been of considerable size, thus in some cases barring potential plaintiffs from taking their case to court. It might be argued that court fees in Denmark have had such proportions that in some cases they might be contrary to EHRC Article 6 on the right of access to court and access to justice. The Civil Justice Council (*Retsplejerådet*, a permanent advisory organ which prepares amendments to Danish procedural law for comprehensive reforms to Danish civil proceedings) has been aware of this, and in one of its reports advised that the fees be reduced, and as part of the court reforms in general this actually happened.

The fees are now calculated as follows (and again it will be remembered, then EUR 1 equals approximately DKK 7.5, so all amounts indicated in DKK must be divided by a factor of approximately 7.5).

---

137. *UfR* 2008:830 V.

First, on instigating the case (i.e., the plaintiff's submission of his summons to the court), the following fee is paid:

- When submitting the plaintiff's summons to the court, at least DKK 1,500 must be paid.
- If the subject of the litigation is not money, or may not be calculated in money, or if the value of the subject of the litigation does not exceed DKK 100,000, the fee is only DKK 750 (instead of DKK 500).

Second, on fixing the date of the final oral hearing (or, if the case is dealt with by the court on a purely written basis, when it has been decided to deal in writing with the case), the supplementary following fee is paid:

- If the subject of the litigation is money, or may be calculated in money, and the value exceeds DKK 50,000, the fee varies from DKK 3,000 to 160,000, depending on the value of the subject of the litigation. The fee cannot exceed DKK 160,000.
- In cases concerning administrative Acts, the fee is DKK 3,000 (instead of the max DKK 160,000).
- All the fees mentioned under this supplementary category are due when the time for the final oral hearing is fixed by the court (or, if the case is dealt with by the court on a purely written basis, when it has been decided to deal in writing with the case), however not earlier than three months before the final oral hearing.
- All the fees mentioned here are, however, annulled if the court receives message from the parties, not later than two weeks before the final oral hearing, that the case is settled out of court by the parties, and that consequently the final oral hearing can be cancelled and the case removed from the court's case list.
- It is obvious that this special provision on 'rebate' in case of an amicable settlement of the case intends to urge parties and counsel to negotiate for at settlement, and if possible to obtain such a settlement in due time before the date fixed for the final oral hearing (all courts being tired of cases which are settled the night before the day fixed for the oral hearing, which will often cause the court to waste a working day).

223. In addition to this, the plaintiff must reckon on legal fees unless conducting his own case. There were standard fees for this for many years. In principle, they were for guidance only, but they were often perceived as rather binding. Higher fees could be charged if, for example, the case was disproportionately complicated or time-consuming, or lower fees if the case was settled before the trial. Danish antitrust authorities challenged the standard fees on the grounds that they constituted a restraint on trade, and a number of years ago, the schedule of recommended fees lapsed in a number of contexts including trial cases.

The lawyer and the client must now instead negotiate the principle of payment from case to case, often taking into consideration the time consumed (of which the lawyer should normally keep a regularly updated record), the result achieved, and the values involved. As already mentioned, the Tariffs agreed by the presidents of the High Courts can give a good, however certainly not binding guidance, cf. above under paragraph 219.

224. If dissatisfied with the fee charged to him by his lawyer (but not, of course, with a court's decision on costs), a client may complain to the Disciplinary Board of the Danish Bar and Law Society (*Advokatnævnet*). Disputes on lawyer's fees can also be taken to court. The Disciplinary Board also hears and decides complaints over an advocate's professional conduct. However, claims for damage must be decided by the courts.

225. When assessing the total risk of going to court, it is necessary to calculate on the cost of two lawyers (own lawyer and the other party's lawyer if the case is lost). Besides this, there is a possibility that the full risk should be multiplied by two, because it may be necessary to conduct the case in two instances (or in three if the case starts in the city court and is eventually granted the right of appeal to the third instance).

If an expert appraiser is appointed, the cost involved must be included in the estimate as well, and it will normally be awarded against the loser.

If several parties are to be included in the case, for example, because the defendant joins a third party to the case by claiming right of recourse against him, the same court fee is payable for the third-party notice as for an ordinary writ, and the legal costs of the third party must also normally be paid by the loser of the case. The total risk in going to court in a case with more than two parties and which may be tried in more than one instance is, therefore, quite considerable.

If, to these costs, the lapse of time is added from the moment when the decision is made to take legal action until judgment or settlement is obtained, there is evidently a long way from one party's assumption of being in the right until he has been given his right with the aid of the court, although the time lapse can be compensated to some extent through the relevant provisions on default interest.

If neither party has its full claim upheld in the judgment, the costs may be divided (cf. section 316 of the *Rpl*), either with a fraction to each party or so that each party pays its own costs ('no order as to costs'): each party pays its own legal costs and plaintiff pays the court costs.

Part VII. Evidence

Chapter 1. Burden of Proof

226. The burden of proof must be placed on the party who has 'acted outside the norm', whether or not he claims to have acted by agreement. Consideration should, however, be given to the party which has easier access to proof. This is particularly so with regard to questions of whether a particular event happened or did not happen. It is normally easier to prove that something did happen than that it did not.[138] Another distinction must be made between the objective and subjective burden of proof, where the objective burden is a kind of obligation to 'convince the court' of a factual proposition which the evidence tends to establish, whereas the subjective burden rests on the party which stands to lose the case at a particular stage in the trial unless he can provide adequate proof for or against.

227. If a party expresses himself in an unclear or ambiguous manner, it may count against him in the court's assessment of what evidence to base the case on. The same applies if a party remains silent unless he has previously challenged the point in question. If, for example, the plaintiff presents his view of a factual event in the writ, and challenges the defendant to declare his agreement with the plaintiff's account, but the defendant omits the question from his statement of defence and does not return to it in the rejoinder, but then returns to the point during the trial – now suddenly wanting to contest it there – the court may, if so requested by the plaintiff, apply the evidence produced in the writ in support of plaintiff's representation of the facts.

This is the so-called prejudicial effect (*fakultativ processuel skadevirkning*), which we meet in many disguises in the civil procedure. The court is not obliged to apply this sanction, but it must assess whether it should be applied. It is thus a facultative or optional sanction and its full designation in Danish is therefore: '*fakultativ processuel skadevirkning*'. If, for example, a company sues another for plagiarizing a design, and the plaintiff requests the defendant to produce further and better particulars with regard to its own development work, but this request is ignored, this may have a prejudicial effect on the defendant's case, on the assumption that if the defendant fails to document his development work, it probably means that no development took place, and this supports the plaintiff's claim of plagiarism.

138. Cf. the most important theoretical contribution in Danish jurisprudence on the allocation of the burden of proof (*bevisbyrden*), E. Tybjerg, *Om bevisbyrden*. København : J. Lund, 1904, p. 59.

Chapter 2. Admissibility of Evidence

228. Anything which is practicably possible to produce in court may be used in evidence, as the principle of free admissibility and assessment of evidence applies. Film, video and tape recordings can thus also be used in evidence. If there is more than one possible way of proving a point, the best possible avenue should be selected. The procedure after the Court Reform 2007/2008 now allows considerably broader scope for giving evidence, for example, by video electronically recorded or transmitted directly during the trial.

The only limitation is that superfluous evidence is not allowed but should be cut off by the court (cf. section 341 of the *Rpl*).

See, e.g., *Telecom A/S*, on an expropriation payment to a farmer in connection with the erection of a 300 m-high TV antenna. Neither the expropriation committee nor the appraisal committee had been willing to make any payment in compensation for the antennae's commanding position and presence, but having inspected the property, the High Court found that compensation was due on this account. A real estate agent and a valuation officer had assessed the loss in the property's commercial value caused by the antenna to be DKK 200,000, but when deciding the question of compensation, the High Court found that it was unable to apply the expert appraisal, which was based on some uncertainty, and applied an estimate instead. The sum to be paid in compensation was set at DKK 100,000.[139]

229. There is 'free' assessment of evidence: cf. the very important principle that 'having regard to what passed during the trial and the testimony, the court decides what facts to follow in its decision' (cf. section 344, subsection 1 of the *Rpl*).

Tax law offers several examples of how the courts have distanced themselves from expert opinions, e.g., in questions concerning the valuation of goodwill in connection with the founding of companies and the question of whether a business is so commercial in nature that a loss incurred should be tax deductible (in contrast to a non-deductible hobby activity). E.g., in a tax case, the High Court followed the expert appraisal and awarded the owner of an art gallery the right of deduction regarding the gallery's continued losses. But four out of the five judges on the Supreme Court bench denied him the right of deduction on the basis, among other reasons, of several years of continued losses with no realistic expectation of making a profit.[140]

'Freedom' is not, however, synonymous with 'arbitrary'. The presumption applies that the judge considers the evidence in the same manner as *another* competent judge would. There is thus a very strong foundation of court practice regarding the standard of evidence, the strength of evidence and burden of proof (cf. immediately below).

As an illustrating example see two cases both concerning fees to the municipality for unlawful parking (a type of case which is in Denmark a civil case, not a criminal case). The High Court stressed that the traffic wardens are 'specially trained for

139. *UfR* 1994:117 V.
140. *TfS* 1999:863 H.

their work', and there is a 'presumption that they will execute their administrative competence as traffic wardens in accordance with the written guidance for such work'.[141]

At the same time, the two cases illustrate the free assessment of evidence because the High Court based its decision in the latter case on the evidence given by the warden, whereas in the former case, the car owner had 'produced such an amount of doubt as to whether his car was parked at the parking space reserved for disabled persons, or outside this parking space' that the fee administered to the car owner by the warden was annulled.

141. *UfR* 2009:1102 Ø and *UfR* 2009:1105 Ø.

Chapter 3. Administration of Evidence

§1. Forced Production of Documents

230. One of the points regarding which civil procedure is rather formal is the area of requests for further and better particulars. Unlike in criminal cases, the object of the court is not to establish the absolute, objective truth (the so-called substantive truth, *materiel sandhed*), but a 'relative', 'subjective' truth (i.e., as established by the parties) based on the case materials supplied to the court by the parties themselves in the form of claims, facts, arguments and evidence.

The parties must therefore give careful consideration to the question of what to produce in order to separately prove what the factual events were. On this point, the civil procedure also differs from administrative procedures, where the inquisitorial principle places the burden of proof solely with the administrative authorities (however, the procedure before some complaint boards is very much like court proceedings).

Requests to the opposite party can, for example, occur in situations where one party presents its view of some aspects of the case, and requests the other party to agree (or disagree, as the case may be) with this view. If the other party does agree, no evidence can or may be called on the question, as the court must not admit superfluous or irrelevant evidence (cf. section 341). It is not the responsibility of the court to verify whether the facts really are as the parties claim.

231. When a party declares his agreement, it is important for the other party to have this confirmed. A statement given in one of the writs is of course firm and binding evidence, but if the statement is given orally during a pretrial hearing or the trial itself, the party for whom the statement is important must ask to have it entered in the court's records. Such a declaration given either in a pleading or during a court hearing is often called a binding deposition (*bindende proceserklæring*), and it will normally be binding on both the present court and any future appeals court. Cf., however, *Børge Christensen*, where the parties had agreed on a method of computing a compensation payment in the High Court, but where the declaration to this effect could be waived in the Supreme Court after a new leading case, *Dansk Eternit Fabrik A/S*,[142] had set new standards for such computations.[143]

232. It is best, of course, if the deposition specifies whether it must also be binding in case of appeal, but it is very rare in practice for such a specification to be given. Agreements entered into under procedural law probably have a less dispositive effect than agreements under private law. If it is clear to the other party that a deposition has been given on the basis of particular case law, and if this law is changed, the declaration may normally be waived if the case is appealed.

This means that one does not need private law's doctrines about unfairness, hardship, etc.; less will do in order to be able to walk away from a 'binding' deposition. However, if the case is settled through amicable agreement, this agreement is of

142. *UfR* 1989:1108 H.
143. *UfR* 1991:153 H.

course exactly as binding as any (other) kind of agreement under private law; such a statement is not given for the purpose of the trial, but on the contrary to end the trial and settle the dispute finally.

233. Now back to the request directed at the other party, urging him to state whether he agrees or not. If the opposite party does *not* agree, each party must consider which of them it will count against if the point is still unclear when the case is set down for judgment. The party who will be prejudiced by the lack of clarity is said to have the burden of proof with regard to the question at issue, and *he* must take steps to produce the requisite proof by calling witnesses, presenting documents, ordering survey with the court's permission, etc.

The statement that a given party carries the burden of proof means that the absence of proof will count against him. It will often be clear, from a law rule applying to the case or the formulation of a contract, which party carries the burden of proof (although the term as such may not have been used). More often, however, the rules must be established on the basis of both theory and practice.

The rules on evidence must normally be established with careful regard to applicable substantive law, such that they support the intentions underpinning the substantive law rules. Cf., for example, *Haubjerg Interiør A/S*, where the Supreme Court held that a frame agreement for a firm to deliver office furniture for Region South Denmark did not imply exclusive rights for the firm, unless the firm could prove this – which it could not.[144]

Much can be read from statutory law and contracts: It certainly can make a difference for the burden of proof, whether a statute, or a contract clause, states that 'if … ', or whether it uses the opposite term: 'unless … '. The condition is turned 180 degrees around, and so will the burden of proof normally also be.

234. If a request to the other party for further and better particulars is not satisfied, the party who made the request may go one step further and apply the *Rpl* rules on discovery of documents (*edition*). This means making a request to the court to order the other party to produce the document (cf. sections 298 and 300).

Thus, e.g., the 'teacher' in the *Pedal-Ove* case took proceedings for defamation, i.e., a civil lawsuit, claiming judgment against the Danish Broadcasting Corporation (DR) and two DR employees, and also requested an order pursuant to section 298, subsection 1, to the effect that DR must produce unedited recordings of the explanations given by two persons. The High Court said 'no' to issuing a discovery order, but the Supreme Court stated: 'As it cannot be denied that the unedited recordings concerning … are important for deciding the case, the Supreme Court orders the Danish Broadcasting Corporation to produce the unedited recordings concerning … 's explanations made in connection with the TV programme "Sentenced for Murder", pursuant to section 298, subsection 1 of the *Rpl.*'[145] Similarly, in a case

144. *UfR* 2009:799 H.
145. *UfR* 1993:170 H.

on the degree of disability caused by an accident, the court ordered the defendant's insurance company to produce the expert medical statement obtained by the company.[146]

235. A request for further and better particulars, and hence also an order for discovery, can also involve evidence which does not in principle concern the case in question but which can impinge on it. Cf., for example, *Center-Pub Tåstrup ApS*, where, in a case on a disproportionate lease, a commercial lessee petitioned for an order for discovery of other leasing contracts in the same shopping centre. This was granted Lessee, but not insofar as Lessor was able to document that a discovery would reveal matters which could be kept secret in the interest of the third party under section 298, subsection 1, cf. section 171 of the *Rpl*, and not insofar as the individual leases were not comparable.[147]

Apart from physical documents, request for discovery can also include electronic materials, including emails.[148]

236. Not every request for discovery is necessarily granted.

See, e.g., *Søren Petersen og Kirsten Petersen*, which rejects the request by some limited partners for the discovery of a legal report which had been prepared by a lawyer for use by the company board after the general meeting had requested the board to investigate a number of issues or to have them investigated. The Supreme Court stressed that the general meetings had made no decision to the effect that the reports should be disclosed to parties other than the boards. The court also cited the fact that the limited partners had not indicated what precise facts they intended to prove through the production of the reports. The court then found no basis for granting discovery.[149]

See also Heini Joensen, on a denial of discovery in connection with a bank's credit rating in a case with a guarantor.[150] The discovery of such internal documents can only be forced in exceptional cases. Cf. also *Erland Thrane*, which unanimously denies disclosure of a management report to the board of a bank on an unsuccessful underwriting of a share issue (commercial underwriting), but where the court, in a dissenting judgment with three votes to two, ordered the bank to produce the management's loans recommendation, among other reasons because the bank managers who had given evidence for use in the Supreme Court case remembered nothing about the loan.[151] A very important decision from the Supreme Court on the matter of discovery is the decision in the case of possible liability for board and management members after the collapse, during the financial crisis, of *Roskilde Bank*,[152] where the court was requested to order the auditors, which were sued for liability together with board and management, to submit all the auditors' internal

146. *UfR* 1999:1443 V.
147. *UfR* 1993:189 Ø.
148. Cf. *UfR* 1998:1613 Ø.
149. *UfR* 1997:837 H.
150. *UfR* 1999:1028 H.
151. *UfR* 1999:1720 H.
152. *UfR* 2015:3319 H.

working papers. The Supreme Court denied issuing such an order, on the grounds that it would constitute 'an inspection-like review' of the auditors' materials.[153]

237. The court does not consider whether the failure to comply with an order for discovery should count against the party until its final deliberation.[154]

The formal procedure here described, involving an order for discovery against the other party, is not by any means the only strategy followed. More often, the party making the request will simply repeat it in his next pleading, perhaps backed up by letter, and he will then, in his final address, ask the court to apply procedural sanctions against the other party with regard to this point (cf. section 298, also section 344, subsection 2). The 'procedural sanctions' in question are *not*, contrary to American procedural law, that the party who does not obey an order for discovery is in 'contempt of court'; it simply means that the court can assume, in the absence of the documents, etc., requested under the discovery, that the facts are as alleged by the party who made the request for discovery.

Section 299, cf. section 300 contains rules governing the third party's duty of discovery. The reason why the duty of discovery is so rarely applied against a *party* is that an order for discovery is unenforceable, and no party is compelled to give evidence. The opposite applies with regard to *third-party* discovery or testimony: the third party has a duty to comply unless exempted or excluded from giving evidence. While the third party *can* thus be compelled to give evidence, a party *cannot*, but the risk that a procedural sanction may be applied often exerts adequate pressure even on the party to ensure compliance.

238. The scope allowed for requests for further and better particulars, and the associated procedural sanctions are not, however, so broad that they allow a party to engage in a major procedural fishing expedition on the other party in the hope that useful evidence may turn up.

This restriction in the scope of such requests sets the somewhat pragmatic approach of Danish law apart from, among others, the far more formalized American procedure. American law provisions on discovery (and the associated disclosure) allow far broader insight into the opponent's documents, correspondence, minutes, etc., and any refusal to comply with disclosure requests can have far-reaching consequences such as losing the case, fines and other sanctions for contempt of court, etc. Before rejecting this as a heavy-handed and formalistic system, it should be remembered that several of the rules have been introduced in order to force the individual party, e.g., the company against the consumer, to provide the other party with lists of all relevant documents in the party's possession.

True, this aspect of the pretrial hearing can appear heavy-handed, but it can be highly effective in preventing a 'weak' party from losing his rights because of lack of evidence. What these rules in effect do is establish a counterpart to the investigative phase of criminal cases. It is not, therefore, entirely without reason that the

153. On this subject *see* Erik Werlauff in *UfR* 2016 B p. 205 et seq.
154. Cf. *UfR* 1999:1475 Ø.

attempts which have been made at creating a common European procedural law operate with quite far-reaching discovery provisions.[155]

It is thus important to note that the Danish procedural provisions on discovery (*edition*) are not nearly of a kind which one meets under, for example, American procedural law. A party cannot forward a 'wholesale' request or go 'fishing' for something to turn up, thereby expecting to receive immense quantities of documents from the other party, and hoping to find, just as the needle in the haystack, *the* document which proves his case. Under Danish procedural law, as in many other countries, the party must specify what document (or kind of document) he is aiming for, and what he expects to prove through that document.

Discovery (*edition*) cannot, for example, be used to provoke the opponent to produce several years' board minutes, etc., but a particular theme may be indicated with a request for the production of minutes (in extract) on this particular theme.

Cf. *Heini Joensen*, where the Supreme Court (*Højesteret)* refused to order Danske Bank to produce some internal credit evaluations in a large case of disappointed investors.[156] In the *Hafnia* case on liability for stock prospectus and stock emission, Danske Bank was ordered to produce parts of its internal board minutes of deliberations, however, anonymized and extracted.[157]

§2. Deposition by Witnesses

239. A very important part of the production of evidence in both civil and criminal proceedings is the questioning of witnesses of the parties in a civil law case and the accused in a criminal case.

Witnesses are compelled to give evidence unless exempt or excluded from this duty.

The *parties* in a civil case are not, however, so compelled, but they will normally decide to do so. If a party refuses to give evidence, it may prejudice his case in the court's assessment of evidence: cf. section 344, subsection 2, of the *Rpl*, the so-called optional prejudicial effect (*fakultativ processuel skadevirkning*– optional, because the court decides freely whether to apply it or not).

Both witnesses and the parties who decide to testify must speak the truth, as they can otherwise be punished for perjury (cf. section 158 of the Criminal Code).

240. The Court Reform 2007/2008 introduced the concept of written statements from witnesses (cf. *Rpl* section 297), either where the parties agree or where the court permits the use of such statement because the court finds it unproblematic.

However, the use of written witness statements does not at all have a proportion under Danish law as we know it under, for example, US or UK procedural law, or

155. Cf. Marcel Storme (ed.), *Rapprochement du Droit Judiciaire de l'Union européenne; Approximation of Judiciary Law in the European Union (EU)*, esp. Ch. 4 of the draft procedural law directive, which is heavily influenced by Anglo-American procedural law on this point, cf. Per Henrik Lindblom in *SvJT* 1996:793 et seq., esp. 820 et seq., and Erik Werlauff, *Common European Procedural Law*. Copenhagen : DJØF Pub., 1999, Ch. 8.

156. *UfR* 1999:1028 H.

157. *UfR* 2002:1734 H.

as we know it from ICC or LCIA arbitration proceedings, where depositions by witnesses play an important (and rather time-consuming) role.

Written witness statements will remain an exception under Danish procedural law. It is suitable for witnesses who are by no means 'main witnesses' of the case, and where the need for cross-examination does not exist. Please observe that a written witness statement is not a supplement to oral evidence from the witness, but that the written statement replaces the oral evidence. Thus, Danish procedural law has no intention of applying the procedure known from US or UK procedural law, where the written statement is only a kind of introduction to oral evidence from the witness, and where the evidence from the witness is a combination of his written and oral statements.

241. Testimony is generally given in the court where the case is heard (cf. section 174 of the *Rpl*).

It is rare, however, for the Supreme Court to hear witnesses or parties. Either the parties merely repeat the relevant parts of testimony given in lower courts, or a new witness, or a witness who was not adequately examined in earlier hearings, must give evidence again, as requested by one of the parties (the so-called production of evidence before an alternative court). Such evidence for use in a civil case in the Supreme Court was previously produced in a city court, but in 1999, the law was changed, and the testimony is now given in the Supreme Court with a senior deputy judge presiding. Senior deputy judges can thus to some extent hear evidence in the Supreme Court in the presence of lawyers having authority (cf. section 4 of the *Rpl*). Decisions of this kind can be appealed to the Supreme Court's Board of Appeal.

A witness permanently residing abroad can be examined there, following a letter of request to the relevant foreign court from the Danish court testing the case, as provided by the Hague Convention of 1905 (cf. section 342 of the *Rpl*). This is also called production of evidence before an alternative court. Community rules – i.e., Regulation no. 1206/2001 on cooperation between courts in the Member States in the field of civil and commercial litigation – provide for mutual assistance in the taking of evidence in cross-national cases, including in the form of video recordings and video-mediated examinations, but unfortunately, Denmark is not yet part of the EU's civil and procedural provisions.

242. Witnesses are summoned by a writ (*vidneindkaldelse*) which must state certain information (cf. section 175 of the *Rpl*). It often happens in civil cases, however, that the lawyer makes less formal arrangements with persons who agree to appear as witnesses, perhaps confirmed by letter, which the witness is asked to sign and return. In this case, the absence of a witness does not, however, incur the legal sanctions which apply to a failure to appear to a formal call. In criminal cases, the formal provisions concerning summoning of witnesses through writs are respected closely.

A witness who fails to appear despite being formally summoned and who has given no notice of absence because of illness or similar, or who refuses to testify although not exempted or excluded from doing so, may, if the court so decides, be fetched by the police, be held liable for damages and (default) fines or taken into custody for up to six months (cf. section 178 of the *Rpl*). The court's decision on the fate of the witness is an order (on a failure to comply with a court order), which must presume that the testimony the witness should have given would have carried considerable value or strength of evidence.[158]

If a witness believes that he or she is exempted or excluded from testifying, the witness must nevertheless appear in court and argue the point, as the decision is made by the court and not by the witness him- or herself (cf. section 179). If an absent witness should appear later, or if it is found that the witness was unavoidably absent, the court can reverse its previous decision.

243. Testimony may normally not be given regarding the general credibility of a witness: thus, the Eastern High Court has refused an expert opinion on whether testator's signature on a will attested by witnesses was genuine because to order an expert opinion would involve accepting testimony as to the credibility of the witnesses to the will, who had already been examined.[159]

§3. Deposition by the Parties

244. The *Rpl*'s rule on the examination of the parties to a case, which states that 'the court may, upon the other party's request, call a party to a personal hearing to answer questions aimed at elucidating the case', bears little relation to the practical reality (cf. section 302, subsection 1, of the *Rpl*). Generally, both parties attend the trial, normally with lawyers who have prepared the cases for them, and in most cases, the parties are more than willing to explain their cases, generally by first answering their own counsel's questions, followed by the questions by counsel for the other party, and perhaps further questions from the court.

The following statement in the *Rpl*, therefore, has far more substance: 'Each party may appear and request a personal hearing. A party who appears in court to be heard shall answer any further questions which the other party or the court may direct to him' (cf. section 303).

245. Despite the provisions cited above, a party cannot be forced to testify in court or to answer individual questions, as a witness can (cf. section 305, also section 178). Whether or not a party wants to testify is therefore in reality voluntary, but if the party refuses to explain a point where the evidence would appear to go against his case, he must generally be prepared to accept that it will count against him. It is a general principle of civil procedure, but not of criminal procedure, that a party's refusal to testify or to produce documentation on points of facts of which he has knowledge or evidence *may* count against him. This prejudicial effect is called optional prejudicial effect (*fakultativ processuel skadevirkning*). It is said to be 'optional' for the court because it is not an automatic consequence. Here too the principle of the court's freedom to assess evidence applies.

158. Cf. *UfR* 1991:123 V.
159. Cf. *FM* 1992:93 Ø.

The fundamental principle of civil procedure with regard to the prejudicial effect in the event of omission to testify and unclear testimony, etc., is so important that it deserves direct quotation from section 344, subsection 2, of the *Rpl*: 'If a party's statements with regard to the facts of the case are unclear or incomplete, or if he omits testifying as to the other party's statements with regard to the same questions or complying with the other party's requests for further and better particulars, the court may hold this against him in its assessment of the evidence. The same shall apply if a party fails to attend a personal hearing to which he has been summoned (cf. section 302) or if he fails to answer a question directed to him under section 302 or 303, or if his answers are unclear or incomplete.'

246. A party may, of course, attend the entire trial. The same applies to the pre-trial hearings, which the lawyers often attend alone, but where the initial section 353 on the preparatory meetings now places considerable demand on attendance, etc., and where the court may, therefore, invite the parties to attend in person. If one of the parties is a legal person, for example, company, foundation or association, the court can invite the party to attend, represented by a person with the requisite authority to make decisions with regard to the case. The underlying assumption is that the section 353 hearing will allow such detailed discussion of the case that a settlement may be reached, which in turn requires that both parties will be able to make binding decisions at the hearing with regard to the case.

Each party hears both the other party's testimony and that of all witnesses (cf. section 305; *see also* section 182). In case this should arouse a suspicion that the parties may conveniently adapt their explanations to suit those of others, I hasten to add that the two parties are the first to be heard, first the plaintiff and then the defendant. The witnesses come after. As mentioned earlier, members of the management or board of a company attending on behalf of a company or other legal persons are deemed to be parties to the case and may, therefore, attend the entire hearing. This also goes for a majority shareholder.

247. If a party decides to testify, he has the same duty to speak the truth as a witness has, and he can therefore be penalized for perjury, *see* section 158 of the Criminal Code (*straffeloven*). A party deciding to testify must therefore be advised of his duty to speak the truth, in the same manner as a witness. After the admonition has been administered by the court, the party is examined by his own counsel, while the cross-examination is performed by counsel for the other party.

§4. Expert Evidence

248. First, it must be emphasized that the use of expert witnesses on both sides plays a minor role under Danish procedural law compared to some other countries, for example, the common law countries. Danish procedural law takes a rather critical stand on a trial where each side is armed with a veritable legion of experts, each given witness evidence in favour of 'his' party. This is not to say that expert witnesses cannot be applied, but they will normally have the attention of the court if they are agreed upon by both parties. This is regulated further under Danish law with effect as from 1 July 2017, cf. below under paragraph 252.

If the parties wish to know what is normal practice and good behaviour for public accountants, they should, *in common and with the acceptance of the court*, address the Legal Opinion Board of FSR – Danish Accountants, and if they wish to obtain an objective medical estimate of a person's physical condition, for example, after an accident, they should in the same way turn to the Danish Forensic Council (*Retslægerådet*). Please *see* further details on expert witness, etc., below under paragraph 250.

If the parties – or rather the party that carries the burden of proof for the presence of faults with delivered goods or services – will need a survey carried out by one or more experts, then again one party should *not* on his own turn to a surveyor, but most raise the question to the court and to the other party (as far as possible already in the preparatory meeting, cf. *Rpl* section 353) to have a survey in the case. When this is allowed by the court, both parties direct written questions to the surveyor (beginning with the so-called theme, *skønstema* or simply: *tema*) written by the party who requests the survey to be carried out.

Also, both parties can demand that the surveyor appears in court at the final oral hearing in order to answer questions from the parties and from the court (the so-called certification, *afhjemling*) – the party against whom the survey report was the 'hardest' of course also being most interested in raising questions at the surveyor's observations and conclusions.

249. Survey (*syn og skøn*) is one or more experts' inspection combined with his or their professional appraisal of how the object inspected compares with certain standards (what is customary, trade practice, market standard, good condition, generally accepted in the profession, etc.). In those exceptional cases where no inspection is required, the term used is 'abstract evaluation'. In the following text, it is assumed that only one surveyor is appointed, which is often the case (if not for other reasons, then for reasons of economy).

As already mentioned, the Court Reform 2007/2008 introduced an option of having the case heard by not just one professional judge in the city court, but by three professional judges, and also the option of introducing two expert judges who (together with one or three professional judges) hear and decide the case. However, the concept of expert judges is not intended to be a substitute for survey or other kinds of factual evidence, cf., for example, *Innotek ApS* on payment for IT programmes delivered at a slaughterhouse in Spain; the High Court did not find sufficient need for expert judges in the case.[160] *See also TfS* 2008:1074 City Court (Kolding) on a tax case with disagreement between the taxpayer and the IRS whether a stud was business or hobby; a survey had been ordered, and if further facts were needed, these could be obtained through the certification (*afhjemling*) during the final oral hearing. However, cf. *Løgten Murer- og Entreprenør A/S*, where the Court of Appeal, contrary to the city court, found a need for two expert judges with building expertise in a case concerning renovation of a private villa.[161]

160. *UfR* 2008:16 V.
161. *UfR* 2010:377 V.

The provisions on the survey were reformed in 2014, thus making the survey easier, simpler and cheaper.

Surveys may be conducted with regard to (just as a few examples):

- the state of a property, a machine or a product batch (e.g., in a case claiming faults);
- the quality and price of a tradesman's work or a set of accounts (e.g., in a case on a tradesman's payment or accountant's fees);
- the market value of goods or services delivered (e.g., in a case on disguised dividend under tax, company or insolvency law);
- the expected profitability of a farm (e.g., in a tax case on the right to deduct losses from a hobby farm: cf. *Steen Ahrenkiel*);[162] or
- the soundness of construction work (e.g., in a case on damage to neighbours), etc.

The expert is requested to compare what he has found by objective investigation (inspection, *syn*) with what he knows subjectively (the appraisal, *skøn*) about a professional matter. Hence, the Danish words for the survey: *syn og skøn*, i.e., inspection and appraisal.

It is the overwhelming stand of Danish jurisprudence that the surveyor cannot, on the other hand, be asked to give an opinion *on a point of law* or with regard to contract or statute interpretation. This delimitation of the expert's competence is based on the traditional distinction between fact and law. The expert may therefore *not* be asked the question of whether there was a *fault* in the object sold on the date of delivery, for in giving an answer to such a question, he would be led to give an interpretation of the parties' agreement, which decides, together with the Purchase Act, whether the object was faulty or free of fault in any legal sense.

The expert *may* be asked, however, whether the object of sale fulfilled certain specifications which appear from the contract, etc., on the date of delivery, or whether the object of sale was suited for a particular application. He may also be asked, for example, 'whether, in the opinion of the expert, it is customary for an object such as the one purchased to deviate by up to x pct. from … ', or: 'Must the object's durability be presumed to be reduced by … .'

250. The *Rpl* contains no special rules on expert statements (*sagkyndige erklæringer*), expert witnesses, etc., but they could be relevant in cases where one party either wants to challenge an expert opinion or where the case is not suited for expert appraisal, for example, because it is a question rather of establishing what the industry practice may be.

Examples of expert appraisals and professional opinions, etc., include:

- In a case concerning the dissolution of a general partnership (or the division of property after divorce), it will be important to establish whether among, for example, doctors, veterinary scientists, accountants, lawyers, etc., there is an established practice with regard to the valuation of goodwill. The question will

162. *UfR* 1994:530 H.

then be referred to the relevant professional body or its committee with responsibility for expert opinions. The same could apply to a tax case.

- In a case brought by or against a lawyer, state-authorized public accountant, certified accountant or real estate agent, it will be important to establish whether the party in question has exceeded the limits of correct professional behaviour (sound legal practice, sound accounting practice, etc.). This question is addressed to the General Council of the Danish Bar and Law Society, the FSR – Danish Accountants, etc.
- In a case brought by or against a bank, it is important whether the bank acted contrary to sound banking practice in its relations with a commercial client, and this question may in certain circumstances be addressed to the Danish Financial Supervisory Authority.
- In a case within a particular industry (the graphics, textile, timber, etc., industry), it is important to establish whether it is customary to charge a particular rate of interest in cases of late payment, in case of a particular deviation from agreed quantities, etc., in case of a special duty of inspection on behalf of the buyer. These questions can be answered by the Confederation of Danish Enterprise (formerly the Danish Chamber of Commerce). Before answering, the Confederation will often enquire from the relevant trade organization.
- In a case on personal injury, it may be important to consult the Forensic Council (although its statements play a bigger role in criminal cases).

251. In the Danish Civil Justice Council (*Retsplejerådet*), it has been discussed whether one should recommend legislator to allow the parties in any civil case, also in the 'smallest' case on defects of a house purchased, to submit expert opinions on fact to the extent that the party wishes. In arbitral cases, this is an option: parties to an arbitral case can freely submit expert opinions just as they like. But the parties to arbitral cases are very often business people or even business undertakings. As such, they should normally not be stopped from submitting whatever they like to submit; the tribunal can handle it. It would seem to look different in private parties' cases on defects, e.g., on the purchase of houses. The Civil Justice Council's recommendation in this area appeared as report no. 1558/2016, and the suggestions in the report were adopted by the legislator and came into force as from 1 July 2017 (*Rpl* section 209a). If the parties agree, the court may accept that each party acquires and submits its own expert opinion on matters of fact; this could happen in larger cases concerning IP rights, larger amounts, etc. If the parties do not agree, the system is as follows: A party is free to submit an expert report which the party has obtained before the instigation of the trial; the other party is then allowed to submit a 'counter-report' which this party has acquired during the trial.

252. Sometimes one party asks a professor of law or other theoretical lawyer for his view on the legal assessment (legal opinion, *responsum*) on the facts of a case. As already mentioned, there has been a restrictive attitude in Danish case law with regard to the submission of legal opinions on Danish law prepared by professors and other expert lawyers, cf. *Blåvandshuk Kommune*.[163]

However, in *Telekæden A/S*,[164] the Supreme Court took a new path, now holding that such legal opinions may be submitted to the court for the sake of the legal argumentation, but not as a proof. This new and refreshing attitude has opened the way to argumentation from either party on the legal aspects of the case, and it has been codified with effect from 1 July 2017 (*Rpl* section 341a §2).

§5. AFFIDAVIT

253. Affidavits, understood as sworn statements, are no longer a feature of Danish procedural law. Before a witness, or a party who has decided to testify, gives evidence, the court impresses upon the person of his obligation to tell the truth (cf. sections 181 and 305 of the *Rpl*): 'The court shall seriously admonish … the witness (party) to speak the truth and impress upon the witness (party) the criminal consequences of perjury.'

254. The opportunity of examining and cross-examining witnesses cannot be replaced by statements of various kinds, but the sheer fact that a document contains explanations by persons whose testimony is sought does not normally prevent the document from being produced. Also, the use of written statements is facilitated after the Court Reform 2007/2008 (cf. *Rpl* section 297), either where the parties agree or where the court permits the use of such statement because the court finds it unproblematic.

See, e.g., Den Danske Bank on the production of a committee report in a case launched by the Faeroe Islands Regional Government against the bank Den Danske Bank for compensation for losses incurred in connection with the island government's purchase of a bank from Den Danske Bank.[165] The report was admitted, which was found not to be contrary to Article 6 of the EHRC. The decision stressed that the defendant would be given full right of defence and the right to present independent evidence.

Depositions for use abroad may be sworn.

§6. INSPECTION BY JUDGE

255. In housing cases, i.e., cases between an owner and a tenant, it often happens that the court (or often just the lay judges alone) inspects the lease (cf. expressly section 112, subsection 3 of the Rent Act). Also, in, e.g., cases involving neighbour law, environmental law, the law of nature protection, etc., inspection on location may be of relevance.

---

163. *UfR* 1996:1293 H, with critical commentary by Lennart Lynge Andersen & Bernhard Gomard in *UfR* 1997 B, 231 et seq.
164. *UfR* 2014:138 H.
165. *UfR* 1999:1549 H.

The *Rpl* has no provisions on inspection in civil law cases. On the other hand, it is assumed in practice that the court can make inspections, for example, of immovable property if the court judges an inspection to be important for its decision in the case. The court can presumably make such a decision ex officio.

Part VIII. Particular Proceedings

256. Certain categories of cases are heard by the ordinary courts under observance of special procedural rules so that the handling of these cases differs somewhat from the above description concerning ordinary civil law cases. This special handling is often termed 'special procedure' in the legal literature.

Common to all these categories is the fact that the parties' freedom to dispose of the subject matter independently is more or less set aside. They are in fact not free so to dispose. It follows that restrictions also apply to the principle that the parties themselves define the issues of the case, and the inquisitorial procedure is proportionately more dominant. Logically, the principle that the parties must provide full and early details of the case is also more restricted in its application. Another common element is the fact that these cases normally end in a model judgment (declaration judgment, *konstitutiv dom*), *see* above under paragraph 165, creating new precedents and obligations either in the relationship between the parties or in relation to the public at large. The final common feature of these cases is the fact that they cannot be joined with ordinary proceedings through accumulation.

257. Marital cases, paternity cases, legal incompetence and guardianship of minors, cases on adoption without parental consent and cases concerning the declaration of death are cases where the parties are not free to dispose of the subject matter. The parties' right to define the issues of the case, their right to freely dispose of its subject matter, and their obligation to provide full and early particulars thus do not normally apply. The rules applying to failure to attend court cannot normally be applied either.

These are city court cases and are normally heard behind closed doors. The court is broadly responsible for elucidating the case (the inquisitorial principle), although this principle is normally reserved for administrative law, not procedural law. The rules on the appointment of lawyers are comprehensive. The parties are not normally ordered to pay costs.

The cases result in what are generally called status judgments in family law.

Status judgments in family law are in principle enforceable. Thanks to their unique quality, the fact that they create a legal status, they do, however, 'enforce' themselves to a large extent: the main content of a divorce order is the divorce. This main content enforces itself. The attending terms, for example, on custody and the joint home, may be enforced via the bailiff's court.

Marital cases (cf. Chapter 42 (sections 448–456) of the *Rpl*) are mainly cases concerning separation and divorce and custody of children. There are, however, important questions connected with marital proceedings which cannot be decided as part of that case: the court cannot make any decision on the couple's joint estate in a divorce case as this question belongs to a different, specialized branch of the city court: the probate division. The question of access to the children for the parent who does not have custody is not decided by the courts either, but by the regional Agency of Family Law (*Familieretshuset*) with possible recourse to the local town court. The vast majority of separations and divorces in Denmark are not granted by the courts but by the Agency of Family Law (*Familieretshuset*) in an administrative divorce certificate (cf. section 42, subsection 2 of the Marriage Act). This is the case where the parties agree on separation or divorce and on the most essential terms.

258. Special rules also apply to the hearing of paternity cases (cf. Chapter 42a (section 456a–r) of the *Rpl* compared with Act on Children's Legal Rights).

Special rules also apply to cases concerning legal incompetence and guardianship (cf. Chapter 43 (sections 457–466) of the *Rpl* compared with sections 6 and 12, nos 2–3, of the Act on Guardianship).

Special rules also apply to the testing of (relatively rare) decisions by the Prefect's Office on adoption without parental consent (cf. Chapter 43b (section 475a–i) of the *Rpl*).

Cases concerning title to property also fall under the category of special procedures (cf. section 476 of the *Rpl*). A judgment conferring title to property is used in cases where the person who believes that he or she is the owner is unable to produce the usual proof of ownership. The judgment then establishes the applicant as the rightful owner of a property, a vessel or a share in a vessel with binding effect on all, i.e., a model example of a judgment which creates law with *erga omnes* effect. A public summons is issued. An application for a public summons will only be granted if the person seeking judgment in the case convinces the court that he or she is the likely owner.

Section 477 of the *Rpl* contains rules on cancellation cases concerning easements and other encumbrances, user rights and rent charges. Judgment in a case of this type cancels such burdens by declaring them 'null and void'. Cancellation cases must be taken to the city court for the jurisdiction in which the property is found. The Act on Cancellation of Securities (*mortifikationsloven*) contains special rules on the cancellation of securities. A security can be cancelled by city court judgment based on a public summons. In principle, the judgment replaces the cancelled security, which is presumed to be destroyed or lost.

Part IX. Seizure for Security and Enforcement of Judgments

Chapter 1. Seizure for Security

§1. Proceedings

259. Interim remedies: seizures (*arrest*) and injunctions (*forbud og påbud*) are characterized by the fact that the applicant does not yet have an enforceable right, *fundament* (no cause of action has yet accrued).

A reform was, as already mentioned, introduced with effect from 1 July 2013, reshaping all the provisions on interim measures. The reform moved the competence in such interim measures from the bailiff's court to the court that has to deal with the merits of the case.

Because the seizure or injunction may therefore later be proved to be unfounded, it is the case almost without exception that in order to be granted seizure or obtain an injunction, the applicant must provide security for any liability for damages in consequence of the seizure or injunction (cf. sections 629 and 415 of the *Rpl*). However, the parties may agree to waive such security, cf. section 415 of the *Rpl.* If at least one of the parties is a consumer, such an agreement cannot be concluded before the dispute has arisen. If both parties are business undertakings (or a public entity), they may enter into such an agreement also before the dispute has arisen. However, the court may on request by exception disregard such an agreement if so especially warranted in the interests of one of the parties.

Strict liability for damages applies if the claim against the debtor is non-existent. It is irrelevant whether the applicant had reasonable cause to believe that he had a claim (e.g., because this was decided in an – appealed – judgment). Many examples may be cited of damages for seizure or injunctions where, in the subsequent confirmatory action, the underlying claim was found not to exist, and where liability for damages was therefore incurred on a strict basis.

As merely one example on the instrument of injunction, *see Toms Chokolade*, where the injunction against the use of a trademark was subsequently found to be unfounded. The trademark was not found to be similar to Tom's trademarks, and the injunction was therefore lifted. The other party was awarded an estimated DKK 150,000 in damages because a batch of chocolate covered by the injunction had to be taken back and destroyed.[166]

166. *UfR* 1993:158 H.

In '*Lokalbanken i Nordsjælland A/S*' ('The Local Bank of Northern Zealand'), the bank was successful in obtaining an injunction against another bank applying the name 'local bank' in a number of towns. The injunction was made, but the latter case on the merits was lost by 'The Local Bank of Northern Zealand' because the name 'local bank' is so common that no exclusive right to such a name can be claimed. The other bank against which the injunction had been made was awarded a compensation of an estimated amount of DKK 250,000.[167]

If the claim did exist but the other conditions for authorizing seizure or injunction were not fulfilled (e.g., because the applicant could have waited for the result of the court case instead of seeking seizure or injunction), liability is merely as per *culpa*. Irrespective of the applicant's cause of action, he is only liable for damages to the extent that the debtor can prove that he has incurred a loss as a result of the seizure or injunction.

On liability for wrongful seizure, *see Knud Kristensen*, where a guarantor for a grocer's overdraft facility paid out the creditor and terminated his credit with the grocer and seized his claim. His (indemnification) claim against the grocer was not due and payable, however, and the entire basis on which the seizure was made therefore missed its mark. The aggressive guarantor was therefore liable for the grocer's losses incurred in the sale of stocks, etc., at a bargain price. The claim did exist, so the guarantor did not incur strict liability. The conditions for authorizing seizure did not exist, and damages were therefore dependent on the existence of *culpa*. On this point, the High Court and the Supreme Court stated that the matter could have been avoided if the guarantor and his advisers had exercised due care.[168]

260. The rules on seizure (*arrest*) are found in sections 627–640 of the *Rpl.* Seizure can only be exercised as security for cash claims. It is a condition that as the applicant does not yet have an enforceable right to his claim, no execution can yet be made with regard to the claim.

Special grounds must also exist for authorizing seizure. There must be a reason to fear that the chance of obtaining cover for the claim will be significantly reduced (section 627), for example, because the defendant is in the process of hiding his assets or moving abroad.

A hotel had reported its female bookkeeper to the police for suspected fraud, and police investigations were underway but could take a long time. The employer feared that the bookkeeper might sell her assets and transfer her property to her mother or brother with whom she lived, but the bailiff's court did not find that there was reason to presume that the hotel's chance of cover for its claim would be significantly reduced if no arrest was made; the application was therefore rejected. The High Court overturned this decision and remitted the case for continued hearing in the bailiff's court with the comment that the information available to the court on the bookkeeper's personal and financial situation was such that the conditions for arrest were met.[169]

167. *UfR* 2007:2392 H.
168. *UfR* 1994:687 H.
169. *UfR* 1993:788 V.

Caution must, however, be exercised before debtor's relations with other EU and EEA countries are considered adequate grounds for arrest. The fact that debtor was in the process of leaving the country (with his assets) was traditionally a strong indication that arrest was justified, but this view must be revised in some cases in light of the EU law prohibition against discrimination on grounds of domicile, nationality, etc. Thus, the fact that a judgment must be enforced in another EU or EEA Member State is not adequate grounds for authorizing seizure: cf. judgment by the European Court in *Mund & Fester and Hatrex*.[170]

261. The bailiff's court performs only a perfunctory test of the existence of the applicant's claim. The risk in this regard thus rests with the debtor (but as noted, with strict liability for the applicant if the claim is proved to be unfounded). The court must, however, make a thorough test of whether there are *grounds* for authorizing seizure, and the burden of proof rests with the applicant on this point (but if he is wrong, he will 'only' be liable under the ordinary *culpa* rule).

The debtor can prevent seizure, or have a seizure cancelled if it has already taken place, by providing security (section 630). This could be a relevant option if an arrest has been made in debtor's property and he then wants to sell it. In that case, there will be two securities, often bank guarantees, deposited in the case: one is the applicant's guarantee deposited as security for the seizure, and the second is the debtor's guarantee deposited as security for release of the seized assets.

The purpose of seizure is first and foremost to ensure that when creditor has later obtained the requisite authority for levying execution, there is still something for execution to be levied on (an object of execution). The institution of seizure can thus be said to form an extension of the protection against debtor's wrongful actions, as it constitutes a criminal offence for debtor to dispose of the seized assets in contravention of the rights of creditor (section 632, subsections 2–3).

262. When an arrest is made of a ship pursuant to the special rules in Chapter 4 of the Merchant Shipping Act (*søloven*), based on the Convention of 10 May 1952 on seizure of ships, the purpose is generally to establish a case of quasi-in-rem jurisdiction because a case against the foreign party may then, as explained above, paragraph 86, be taken to the Danish court where the ship was arrested (cf. sections 246a and 247, subsection 1, last sentence). Since, according to these rules, the arrest of ships is understood as a lien on a ship present where the arrest was made, an arrest, in reality, is rather an order preventing the ship from continuing its voyage. The operating loss, etc., involved in having a ship out of action will often be enough reason for the debtor (shipping line) to prevent the arrest by depositing a guarantee. Arrest of a vessel is a unique legal institution which on the one hand refers to the *Rpl*'s rules on seizure for complementation (cf. section 96 of the Merchant Shipping Act), but which on the other hand is an independent concept in law with its own norms, having priority even to the Brussels I Regulation (cf. *Rpl* section 247).

263. The fact that seizure is relatively little used now is also due to the fact that a creditor will normally not achieve very much through it. It even has the negative

170. C-398/92. *See also* Erik Werlauff, *Common European Procedural Law*, 25 et seq. and 228.

effect that it can 'alert' other creditors and show them where execution may be levied, as assets seized are not protected against debtor's other creditors. A seizure is therefore in effect performed to the advantage of all the debtor's creditors, cf. *Kreaturhandler Skærbæk*[171] with note 2 and *Styhr & Kjær*.[172] The point is that any execution levied against the seized assets assumes the level of ranking previously held by the seizure. This also applies if the execution is levied by another creditor than the one who seized the assets in the first place.

In most cases where execution is levied by a third party, the seizure will thus move down the order of ranking. If the seized asset has been sold, the seizure vanishes entirely if the execution is levied by a third party. If debtor is declared bankrupt or dies, the seizure lapses automatically (section 31, subsection 3, of the Bankruptcy Act, and section 10, subsection 4, of the Probate Act). In this case, retention of the asset which the seizure ensured has also benefited all creditors. If the estate is later handed over for administration out of court, if undivided possession of the estate is retained or if it is handed over to the surviving spouse, the seizure becomes fully effective as if it had never been interrupted.

A seizure is, however, protected against bona fide assignees. If a debtor sells the seized asset, buyer must respect the arrest if the creditor has protected his interest by the requisite act of perfection (for immovable property: entry in the land register: cf. section 1 of the Land Registration Act. For negotiable securities: deprivation of the right of disposal: cf. section 22 of the Instruments of Debt Act). A new mortgage creditor must also respect the arrest (in contrast to judgment creditors).

§2. Judicial Review

264. It may be that a case on the substance, i.e., concerning the right allegedly violated, is already pending before a Danish or a foreign court, or before an arbitral tribunal in Denmark or abroad. If so, the case pending on the substance is, of course, expanded to also include the interim measures which have been obtained. If such case on the substance is not pending, such a case must be instigated as a civil action in Denmark or abroad, or as an arbitral case in Denmark or abroad, as the case may be. The case on the substance must then be commenced within seven days (seizure) and fourteen days (injunction) if the parties do not agree otherwise (section 425).

Even if the seizure is followed by confirmatory action, the bailiff's decision on whether to seize or not to seize assets can be appealed (section 640). As the High Court should in principle decide the appeal on the same basis as the bailiff's court, an appeal is not particularly appropriate if the dispute concerns creditor's claim, as the bailiff's court can only make a summary test of this issue.

As the provisions on *injunction* were reformed with effect from 1 July 2013, the provisions on judicial review in injunction cases were also reformed. The judicial review can now be an arbitral proceeding if the parties have agreed on that in their contract, etc. Or it could be a court case that has already been instigated. Again, please observe that injunction is, as from 1 July 2013, no longer a matter for the bailiff's court but for the ordinary courts.

171. *UfR* 1946:340.
172. *UfR* 1975:965 V.

Chapter 2. Enforcement of Judgments

§1. Enforcement of Domestic Judgments

I. Proceedings

265. The bailiff's court (*fogedretten*) only swings into action in response to an application. The court fixes the time and place for enforcement (cf. section 487, cf. section 489, on jurisdiction). Most enforcement procedures take place in the bailiff's office simply to save resources.

Execution can be levied if either the debtor or the asset to be seized is present. Execution can, however, be levied against a mortgage deed in fixed property in the bailiff's office even if debtor is not present (cf. section 495). Execution cannot be levied against property not located in Denmark.[173]

The court may decide that proceedings should continue to the debtor's address (*udkørende fogedforretning*), for example, at the debtor's home or business address or the place where the object to be seized is located.

266. If a debtor fails to appear after having been served with a lawful summons, the bailiff's court can issue an order for police arraignment (cf. section 494). Police arraignment is a form of arrest. The police will in practice attempt to convince the debtor to appear of his own accord. If this fails, he will be picked up by the police and then retained in the local prison or the police station until he can be arraigned in court.

These cases are humiliating for the debtors involved and a burden on police resources. No arraignment is arranged in very small cases or in cases where the bailiff assesses that there are no assets to seize. Proceedings at a debtor's address are an alternative to police arraignment. If the court refuses to order police arraignment, the creditor will normally be able to demand proceedings at the address instead. If, on the other hand, creditor requests proceedings at the address, the bailiff will not normally be able to decide on police arraignment instead unless specific circumstances in the case make it advisable not to grant the request, cf., e.g., *Køkkenland A/S*.[174]

A forced sale may normally be requested immediately after the enforcement proceedings, but the sale may generally not be held until a period of four weeks has elapsed after the enforcement (cf. section 542).

II. Judicial Review

267. One very important point is that the bailiff's court cannot decide whether a judgment or order is correct (cf. section 501, subsection 2). This also applies to

173. Cf. *FM* 1996:62 Ø.
174. *UfR* 1991:740 Ø.

judgments from the other EU Member States submitted for enforcement in Denmark under the Brussels I Regulation. A party who is dissatisfied with a court decision must appeal the decision. He cannot instead express his dissatisfaction by making objections in the bailiff's court.

It is a matter of dispute whether the bailiff's court, in quite exceptional circumstances, can overturn a judgment because it rests on a blatantly obvious mistake. It appears to have happened only once, cf. *Kjolesalonen 'Hansa'* where, in naming debtor, the judgment confused a woman with her ex-mother-in-law.[175]

Subsequent grounds of discharge include objections that the claim has been discharged through payment, offsetting, barring of claims (in consequence of a negative prescription, mainly with regard to deceased estates), or statutory limitations. All these examples concern objections with regard to circumstances which have arisen *after* the grounds for authorizing enforcement were established. Practical reasons speak in favour, of course, of the bailiff's court deciding objections of this nature. To this should be added that they are typically relatively simple to decide.

268. Disputes in the bailiff's court will, of course, relate either to fact or law. The court must in principle decide legal disputes to the same extent as other courts, also in cases where complicated legal questions may arise of a kind (perhaps even involving constitutional or EU law) which may be less appropriately decided in the course of enforcement proceedings. If the interpretation of EU law or its applicability in the case is at stake, the bailiff can submit the problem as a preliminary question to the European Court: cf. Article 267 EEC.

If, because of the DKK 20,000 limit (cf. immediately below, before 2014 a DKK 10,000 limit), the bailiff's decision cannot be appealed to the High Court without permission from the Appeals Permission Board, the bailiff is the court of last instance (as the option of applying for permission to appeal an interlocutory order does not apply to cases below this limit). The bailiff then has a duty to submit the question to the European Court, but if EU law is clear, the bailiff merely has the right, not a duty, to submit questions (the *acte claire* principle).

See on this *Master Food A/S* where a bailiff's court in a case on enforcement of an AMBI claim (AMBI being a special Danish employer tax, found by the European Court to contravene EU law after some years of 'active service') attempted to refer the case to the High Court because of its general importance, but where the High Court returned the case to the bailiff's court to be tried there on its merits on the grounds that the section 227s scope for referral (referral from city court to High Court) did not apply to proceedings in the bailiff's court. The bailiff thus failed in his attempts, by both rejection and referral, to escape having to do battle with the Sixth European VAT directive![176]

269. The bailiff can refuse to hear evidence which, because of its extent or nature or for other special reasons, should be given in an ordinary court case (section 501, subsection 4).

175. *UfR* 1935:1124 Ø.
176. *UfR* 1989:973 Ø.

The bailiff's court decides disputes through the issuing of orders (cf. section 501, subsection 5) which may be appealed to the High Court, although subject to the DKK 20,000 limit (before 2014 a DKK 10,000 limit), which also applies to the authorization of execution (but not to other enforcement proceedings), also with respect to decisions on costs (cf. section 503, subsections 2–3 and section 584, subsection 2). Orders which cancel costs (i.e., let each party pay its own costs) can always be appealed.

Costs may be awarded to and against the parties in a bailiff's case (cf. section 503 for more).

§2. Recognition and Enforcement of Foreign Judgments

I. Rules Applicable in the Absence of a Treaty

270. Foreign judgments which are not governed by one of our conventions on mutual recognition and enforcement are not enforceable in Denmark. It will, therefore, be necessary to take proceedings to claim recognition of the foreign judgment in Denmark, the so-called *exequatur* endorsement, and the Brussels I Regulation does not apply in such cases.

271. Court proceedings for the recognition and enforceability of a foreign judgment which is *not* automatically recognized in Denmark under one of our conventions may in principle include the hearing of evidence about circumstances which were finally decided in the judgment, and which are therefore deemed to be enforceable in the country where the judgment was given. This took place in a case on recognition of a Turkish judgment on custody of a child. The Danish case tested whether, and confirmed, the Turkish father who had been granted custody in the judgment in Turkey had actually exercised custody while the child was in Turkey.[177]

II. International Treaties

272. Judgments from the other Scandinavian countries are generally enforceable in Denmark.

The same applies to judgments from countries covered by the Brussels I Regulation and the San Sebastian and Lugano Conventions. The important factor in recognition is not whether the foreign court relied on the Regulation or not for its competence. This is the case even if the foreign court made a procedural error in considering only its own national procedure and not the Brussels I Regulation (cf. *Hotel International*, – a German court cited only the *Zivilprozessordnung*, not the Regulation).[178]

---

177. *TFA* 1999:123 Ø (= *UfR* 1999:499 Ø).
178. *UfR* 1990:479 V.

Only where it is evident that the court ignored the Regulation's mandatory protective rules on jurisdiction in consumer or insurance matters, or if the judgment's enforcement would contravene the *ordre public*, must enforcement be denied. According to the ECJ's judgment in *Gambazzi v. DaimlerChrysler*,[179] it may, for example, be contrary to *ordre public* that the defendant was excluded from participating in his own litigation because he had shown 'contempt of court' by denying obeying some of the court's orders.

With the introduction of the Brussels I Regulation's rules on enforcement of judgments from other European countries, what has been termed the 'free movement of judgments across national borders' has been achieved. Not only are these foreign judgments thus enforceable in Denmark, both in terms of issue estoppel and cause of action estoppel (a new case on the same matter between the same parties will be denied: *ne bis in idem*, not twice the same: cf. Article 25), they are also enforceable. New claims and allegations in a new case between the same parties will, however, often lead to the conclusion that the new case is not identical to the earlier case, and consequently that the principle of *ne bis in idem* does not apply. *See*, for example, *Scandinavian Car Styling*, where a judgment pronounced by an Italian court was no obstacle to a new case in Denmark (where there was venue because of a Danish agent fulfilling his tasks here), the first case only deciding whether there was a sole distributorship, the second case being about the parties' economic claims.[180]

Costs are also enforceable, even if they are not set by the court itself as in Denmark, but fixed by an administrative decision, as applies, for example, under German law.

Not only judgments in civil cases but also decisions concerning taxes, VAT and other duties owed to public authorities in other EU countries are enforceable in Denmark, cf. EU Directive 76/308 on mutual assistance by the enforcement of certain claims. No separate (foreign or Danish) judgment is demanded in order to enforce such decisions, cf., e.g., *Told- og Skatteregion Sønderborg* recognizing enforcement in Denmark of a German administrative decision concerning duties for having smuggled cigarettes into Germany. The administrative decision from German tax authorities had been sent to, and was received by, a Danish citizen who was a passenger in the car in which the cigarettes were smuggled.[181]

273. The bailiff can request a translation of a judgment from another European Member State. The request may be for a certified translation (in contrast to an 'informal' translation), but no legalization of the translation via the Ministry of Foreign Affairs may be required. The bailiff may also request a translation of the acknowledgement of service. The bailiff may not review the case as to its substance.

274. Under the terms of the Regulation, it is a condition for the enforcement of judgments in default that the defendant was validly served with the writ, so that defendant had a reasonable opportunity to defend his interests in the proceedings.

179. C-394/07.
180. *UfR* 2008:1753 V.
181. *UfR* 2002:2008 H.

However, as numerous objections were heard under the Brussels Convention, the relevant objections from the debtor have been narrowed on two important points in the Brussels I Regulation (Article 34, no. 2), compared to the Convention (Article 27, no. 2):

- The Regulation has added the words: 'unless the defendant has not taken steps in order to contest the judgment, although he has an opportunity to do so', thereby reducing the possible objections coming from defendants.
- Whether the initial document (the writ) was validly served under national procedure is no longer important. The important element is whether it was served in such good time and in such a manner that the defendant was able to defend his interests in the case.

275. Enforcement under the terms of the Regulation is conditional upon its being enforceable in the country where it was given. Enforcement is not prevented, on the other hand, by the judgment being appealed, but debtor can then ask to have the enforcement proceedings stayed: cf. Article 46, subsection 1.

276. Most foreign arbitration decisions in disputes of a commercial nature (quite a broad concept in this context) are enforceable in Denmark (cf. sections 38–39 of the Arbitration Act). Denmark has bound itself to this under the New York Convention of 1958.

Part X. Arbitration

277. Having lagged behind in its arbitration rules for thirty years, Denmark – as from 1 July 2005 – again became an attractive country in which to conduct arbitration. Denmark follows in all major questions the framework and contents of the United Nations Commission on International Trade Law (UNCITRAL) Rules. The Arbitration Act of 2005 (hereinafter called 'AA') provides a very broad framework for party autonomy.

Chapter 1. Arbitrability

278. Only such legal matters in which the parties are free to make agreements can be subject to arbitration, cf. AA section 6. For example, a divorce cannot be agreed through arbitral proceedings. A consumer will be bound by an arbitral agreement provided that the agreement was made between the parties after the disagreement has arisen, cf. section 7, subsection 2, AA.

279. The fact that questions of mandatory provisions under public law are part of the litigation does not prohibit it from being arbitrated. E.g., antitrust matters can be decided by the arbitrators, and thus a party alleging that his obligations under a contract are prohibited by antitrust law can submit such allegations before the arbitral tribunal.[182]

182. On this subject, *see* Erik Werlauff, *Private Arbitration on Incidental Public Law Issues*, European Business Law Review 565 et seq. (2009).

Chapter 2. Arbitration Agreement and Party Autonomy

280. The party autonomy starts with the arbitration agreement itself. The arbitration agreement is often contained in a clause in a larger contract between the parties, being it a sales agreement, an agreement on distributorship, a shareholders' agreement, or other kinds of commercial contract. The parties can also agree on arbitrating a specific dispute which has already arisen between them (as already mentioned, a consumer can only bind himself or herself through an arbitral clause which he or she has agreed to after a specific dispute has arisen).

281. The party autonomy continues with the option to agree on various other questions concerning the arbitral case. E.g., the parties can agree that they and the arbitral tribunal are to apply digital means of communication, e.g., emails with attached files. There is, of course, nothing to prevent the parties from having agreed in advance in the arbitration clause that digital media are a valid method of communication between the parties, between the parties and the arbitral tribunal, and between the arbitrators.

282. Also, the language of the court is subject to party autonomy (section 22 of the AA). If the parties do not exercise their right in this respect, the court will decide the language of the arbitration proceedings. The choice of language also applies to written submissions, oral hearings, awards, other decisions, etc.

283. Furthermore, the parties may finally also set the time limits for submission of the individual pleas during the preparation of the case, but if they have not exercised their right of autonomy in this respect, the court will make the decision (section 23, subsections 1–2). We are probably here entering an area where it will be better for the parties to leave the question to the best judgment of the court.

284. Party autonomy also applies to the choice of law under international law (section 28, subsection 1, 1st sentence, of the AA). There is nothing to prevent a Danish arbitral tribunal from applying foreign law if the parties so decide. Unless the parties decide otherwise, the reference to the law of another country does not include a reference to that country's rules on conflict of law (section 28, subsection 1, 2nd sentence). In other words, the Act's (dispensable) principle is that the choice of international law does not imply any renvoi. It would hardly be appropriate to exercise one's party autonomy on this point. A renvoi clause can sometimes lead to insurmountable problems. If the parties' contract does not include a choice of law agreement, the arbitral tribunal will make the decision under the rules of international law (section 28, subsection 2).

285. It is well known that considerations of equity are a major component in every opinion or award given by an arbitral tribunal. However, there is a considerable difference in whether such considerations are allowed to influence the result of the case within the framework of applicable law, or whether the case is decided *ex aequo et bono*. As was also assumed prior to the adoption of the AA of 2005, explicit authorization is required for the arbitral tribunal to decide the case according to equity (section 28, subsection 3). The same applies if the parties wish to use their autonomy to empower the arbitral tribunal to decide disputes of interests as such (understood in contrast to or as a supplement to disputes of rights). Decisions on disputes of interests can involve deciding the question of price change, decisions under hardship clauses, etc.

286. Explicit authority is also required for the arbitral tribunal to decide a case according to *lex mercatoria*, i.e., according to the principles of law that are common for modern industrial countries and without applying the substantive rules of any given country. When referring to such principles, the tribunal will assume that the parties have meant the UNIDROIT Principles of international commercial contracts, in its latest version.

287. The parties can also agree on the place of arbitration under section 20 of the AA. If they do not, the court makes the decision, and it may meet for questioning, deliberation, etc., wherever convenient. An arbitration agreement which specifies the place of arbitration can contribute to establishing the requisite balance in the dispute: arbitration in country X may thus be tied to the use of country Y's language, and that meetings must be held in country Y. If a Danish party is involved in French arbitration, that party may actually feel that a fair balance has been achieved if the meetings are held in Denmark.

Chapter 3. The Composition of Arbitral Tribunal

288. The parties are free to determine the number of arbitrators, cf. section 10, subsection 1, AA. Failing such determination, the number of arbitrators shall be three, cf. section 10, subsection 2, AA. So again, there is quite a considerable degree of party autonomy when it comes to the question of the composition of the arbitral tribunal.

289. The parties are also free to specify how the arbitrators should be appointed (section 11, subsection 1). If no such agreement has been made, each party will appoint one arbitrator, and the two arbitrators thus appointed jointly appoint the third. The Act provides rather long deadlines: thirty days for the appointment of the parties' own arbitrator and another thirty days for the appointment of the umpire arbitrator (section 11, subsection 2). It may be advised to use party autonomy to maintain this traditionally well-functioning appointment system while reducing the deadlines.

290. The parties' autonomy in deciding the composition of the arbitral tribunal can also be used to specify the procedure for handling objections against an arbitrator (section 13, subsection 1, of the AA). If the parties fail to exercise their right of autonomy on this point, the Act prescribes that the objection must be launched within fifteen days of the objecting party's having been advised of the arbitrator's appointment, and the reasons for the objection must be given. Unless the arbitrator withdraws voluntarily or the other party agrees that his/her appointment should be withdrawn, the arbitral tribunal decides whether the objection should be upheld.

291. One of several ways of specifying the 'procedure' for handling a case is to agree that the arbitration case must be submitted to a named *institute of arbitration*, for example, The Danish Institute of Arbitration (*Voldgiftsinstituttet*). Such a provision naturally also implies the acceptance and specification of the procedural rules of that institute. By doing this, the parties will have applied the autonomy made available to them in section 19 in quite considerable detail.

Please *see* the Institute's website for further information on the rules of procedure, costs, etc.: http://www.voldgiftsinstituttet.dk.

Chapter 4. Interim Measures and Preliminary Awards

292. The ordinary courts may, at the request of a party, grant an order for an interim measure of protection or enforcement even if the parties have agreed to submit the dispute to arbitration, cf. section 9 AA.

293. The arbitral tribunal may, at the request of a party, order any party to take such interim measure of protection as the arbitral tribunal may consider necessary in respect of the subject matter of the dispute, cf. section 17 AA, which is totally inspired by the UNCITRAL Model Law. The arbitral tribunal may require any party to provide appropriate security in connection with such measure.

Chapter 5. Conduct of Arbitral Proceedings

294. An arbitration case is deemed to have commenced when the defendant receives a written request for the dispute to be settled by arbitration (section 21, subsection 1, of the AA), but the parties may also use their right of autonomy to decide this point differently. It goes without saying that this question is important for deciding lis pendens, period of limitation, prejudgment interest, etc., so the point is of more than theoretical interest. It is undeniably a modest demand to make of the plaintiff that all he needs to do is to produce and forward a written request for arbitration in order for the action to be deemed to have been instigated. The party autonomy offered under section 21 could therefore well be used with advantage to agree that the request will have the above foreclosing effect only if accompanied by a statement of claim and the exhibits on which it relies.

Chapter 6. Arbitral Award

295. The arbitral award shall be made in writing and shall be signed by the arbitrator(s), cf. section 31, subsection 1, AA. In arbitral proceedings with more than one arbitrator, the signatures of the majority of all members of the arbitral tribunal shall suffice, provided that the reason for any omitted signature is stated. The award shall state the reasons upon which it is based unless the parties have agreed that no reasons are to be given (or the award is an award on agreed terms under section 30 AA), cf. section 31, subsection 2. The award shall state its date and the place of arbitration, cf. section 31, subsection 3, and the award shall be deemed to have been made at that place. After the award is made, a copy signed by the arbitrators shall be delivered to each party, cf. section 31, subsection 4. This provision is taken very seriously by arbitral tribunals in Denmark, and thus a photocopy to each party will not suffice; each party is entitled to receive a sample of the award bearing the original signatures of the arbitrators.

296. The arbitration tribunal decides any questions of its own jurisdiction, including objections against the existence or validity of the arbitration agreement (section 16, subsection 1, 1st sentence). In other words, an arbitral tribunal under Danish law is one of the institutions which have 'competence-competence'.

The principle of separability has now finally reached the statute book in the AA: an arbitration clause which is part of a contract is deemed in terms of the arbitral tribunal's competence to be a separate agreement independent of the other parts of the contract. A decision by the arbitral tribunal that the contract is invalid does not, therefore, automatically imply that the arbitration clause is also invalid (section 16, subsection 1, 2nd and 3rd sentences). This principle, which Denmark shares with most other countries, thus rids the arbitral tribunal of the tautology which would arise if a decision on the invalidity of the contract automatically implied the invalidity of the arbitration clause, and thus rescission of the competence on which the decision was based.

If the arbitral tribunal makes a separate decision on jurisdiction, the Act provides a thirty-day limit for submitting the decision to the courts for testing (section 16c, subsection 3, of the AA). This provision cannot be dispensed with by agreement (section 2, subsection 2).

Similarly to the situation applying in other countries, the AA now provides (in section 17) that the arbitral tribunal may order a party to take whatever 'interlocutory steps' may be necessary, possibly against providing security. Such orders are not enforceable and can therefore not be compared with an injunction proper (cf. the UNCITRAL Arbitration Rules).

297. Costs fall due for payment thirty days after the case is closed (section 33, subsection 1). The parties are jointly and severally liable (section 34, subsection 2). The costs can be tested separately in court (thirty-day time limit) (section 34, subsection 3). The arbitral tribunal divides the costs between the parties (section 35, subsection 1). The court can also impose costs on a party (section 35, subsection 2).

298. The tribunal (or the institute, if the case is treated under an institute, e.g., The Danish Institute of Arbitration, Voldgiftsinstituttet, in Copenhagen) may demand security from the parties (section 36, subsection 1). The court can close the case if security is not provided (section 36, subsection 1). The other party can, however, elect to provide the entire security (section 36, subsection 2). If the other party does not choose to do so, and the court closes the case, the other party can take the case to the ordinary courts.[183]

299. And what are then the costs for conducting an arbitral case in Denmark? In the so-called good old days, one simply took 3%–4.5% of the disputed amount for a three-person arbitral court, and split this salary between the three arbitrators, perhaps with a little overweight to the chairman of the tribunal. Nowadays, arbitration has become cheaper, and consideration is taken to: (1) the disputed amount; and (2) the difficulty and length of the case. If the arbitral case is under The Danish Institute of Arbitration (Voldgiftsinstituttet) in Copenhagen, the cost provisions of the institute are binding on the parties as well as the arbitrators. If the arbitral case is a so-called ad hoc case, i.e., outside the institute, the arbitrators will nevertheless take the institute's cost provisions as their guideline. One can agree with the arbitrators on certain cost rules, e.g., an hourly rate, but this rarely happens in practice.

300. Please go to the homepage of the institute, http://www.voldgiftsinstituttet.dk, choose English as your language, and go to the cost calculator. Here, you can fill in the amount, in DKK or EUR, and see what the cost will be (or rather: the range from a minimum to a maximum, with an average that will offer some guidance). Please observe that the cost calculator will tell you the cost: (a) for a case with three arbitrators; and alternatively (b) the cost for a case with only one arbitrator. Please also observe that one arbitrator is, for simple cost reasons, the main rule now, but that the specific arbitral clause of the case can provide for three arbitrators.

301. However again, in cases where the parties have agreed in the arbitral clause that the case is to be decided by three arbitrators, they can always agree appositely, i.e., they can agree that this specific case should only be decided by one arbitrator. Also, some arbitral clauses state that if the value of the case is less than (e.g.,) EUR 100,000, the case shall be decided by just one arbitrator and that cases with a value of more than EUR 100,000 must be decided by a panel of three arbitrators. Again, the principle of party autonomy prevails.

---

183. Cf. *UfR* 2009:248 Ø.

Chapter 7. Recourse Against Arbitral Award

302. With the Danish Arbitration Act (AA) as from 2005, it was intended to ensure that as a very strong main rule, arbitral awards will stand. Thus, the possibilities of successfully contending an arbitral award are limited. Anyone who is familiar with the UNCITRAL Rules, and the UNCITRAL Model Law, will immediately recognize these rules in the Danish provisions, cf. section 37 of the Danish AA. If you have Article 34 of the UNCITRAL Model Law in front of you, you will recognize its provisions almost word by word in the Danish section 37 of the AA.

303. An arbitral award may be set aside *only if* (section 37, subsection 2, of the AA):

(1) the party making the application furnishes proof that:
   (a) a party to the arbitration agreement was, under the law of the country in which that party was domiciled at the time of conclusion of the contract, under some incapacity, or the said agreement is not valid under the law to which the parties have subjected it or, failing any indication thereon, under Danish law;
   (b) the party making the application was not given proper notice of the appointment of an arbitrator or of the arbitral proceedings or was otherwise unable to present his or her case;
   (c) the award deals with a dispute not contemplated by or not falling within the terms of the submission to arbitration, or contains decisions on matters beyond the scope of the submission to arbitration; or
   (d) the composition of the arbitral tribunal or the arbitral procedure was not in accordance with the agreement of the parties or with this Act; or
(2) the court finds that:
   (a) the subject matter of the dispute is not capable of settlement by arbitration; or
   (b) the award is manifestly contrary to the public policy of Denmark.

You will recognize the UNCITRAL Model Law in all this; Denmark is, as from 2005, an UNCITRAL country.

304. If a ground for setting aside concerns only part of the arbitral award, only that part may be set aside, cf. section 37, subsection 3, AA.

305. An application for setting aside may not be made after three months have elapsed from the date on which the party making that application had received the award, cf. section 37, subsection 4, AA.

306. The court, when asked to set aside an award, may, at the request of a party, suspend the setting aside proceedings for a period of time determined by it in order to give the arbitral tribunal an opportunity to resume the arbitral proceedings or to take such other action as in the arbitral tribunal's opinion will eliminate the grounds for setting aside, cf. section 37, subsection 5, AA.

307. Where an arbitral award is set aside, the arbitration agreement shall, unless otherwise agreed by the parties or inconsistent with the judgment setting aside the arbitral award, again become effective, cf. section 37, subsection 6 AA.

308. Within thirty days of receipt of the award, a party may request the arbitral tribunal to correct in the award any errors in computation, any clerical or typographical errors or any errors of similar nature, cf. section 33, subsection 1, AA. The request shall also be communicated to the other party. If the arbitral tribunal considers the request to be justified, it shall make the correction within thirty days of receipt of the request. The arbitral tribunal may correct any error of the type referred to above on its own initiative within thirty days of the date of the award, cf. section 33, subsection 2, AA.

309. Within thirty days of receipt of the award, a party may request the arbitral tribunal to make an additional award as to claims presented in the arbitral proceedings but omitted from the award, cf. section 33, subsection 3, AA. The request shall also be communicated to the other party. If the arbitral tribunal considers the request to be justified, it shall make the additional award within sixty days of receipt of the request.

Chapter 8. Recognition and Enforcement of Awards

310. An arbitral award, irrespective of the country in which it was made, shall be recognized as binding and shall be enforced in Denmark in accordance with the provisions of the Rpl on the enforcement of judgments, cf. section 38, subsection 1, AA. The party relying on an award or applying for its enforcement shall supply a duly certified copy of the award, and of the arbitration agreement if the agreement is in writing. The documents shall, if necessary, be accompanied by a duly certified translation into Danish, cf. section 38, subsection 2, AA. Recognition or enforcement of an arbitral award, irrespective of the country in which it was made, may be refused only:

(1) at the request of the party against whom it is invoked, if that party furnishes proof that:
   (a) a party to the arbitration agreement was under the law of the country in which that party was domiciled at the time of conclusion of the contract, under some incapacity, or the said agreement is not valid under the law to which the parties have subjected it or, failing any indication thereon, under the law of the country where the award was made;
   (b) the party against whom the award is invoked was not given proper notice of the appointment of an arbitrator or of the arbitral proceedings or was otherwise unable to present his or her case;
   (c) the award deals with a dispute not contemplated by or not falling within the terms of the submission to arbitration, or it contains decisions on matters beyond the scope of the submission to arbitration;
   (d) the composition of the arbitral tribunal or the arbitral procedure was not in accordance with the agreement of the parties or with the law of the country where the arbitration took place;
   (e) the award has not yet become binding on the parties or has been set aside or suspended by a court of the country in which, or under the law of which, that award was made; or
(2) if the court finds that:
   (a) the subject matter of the dispute is not capable of settlement by arbitration under Danish law; or
   (b) the recognition or enforcement of the award would be manifestly contrary to the public policy of this country.

311. If a ground for refusing recognition or enforcement concerns only part of the arbitral award, only that part may be refused recognition or enforcement, cf. section 39, subsection 2, AA. If an application for setting aside or suspension of an award has been made to a court referred to in subsection 1, no. 1(e), the court where recognition or enforcement is sought may adjourn its decision and may also, on the application of the party claiming recognition or enforcement of the award, order the other party to provide appropriate security, cf. section 39, subsection 3, AA.

312. Again, you will recognize the UNCITRAL Model Law in all this; as mentioned several times, Denmark is, as from 2005, an UNCITRAL country.

Part XI. Mediation

Chapter 1. Legislation/Definitions

313. Many arbitration clauses in Danish contracts will today be completed by a clause on mediation. Mediation has, rightfully so, become popular, and plays a significant role both in connection with traditional court cases and in connection with arbitral clauses and cases. In Denmark, three kinds of mediation are currently offered:

(1) Mediation offered by all Danish city courts when cases are instigated, provided that the case is suitable for mediation. This kind of mediation is named *retsmægling* (= court mediation), and the costs for the mediator are carried by the state if the court accepts the case to be mediated.
(2) Mediation offered by the Danish arbitral institution Voldgiftsinstituttet (The Danish Institute of Arbitration) as an alternative or a supplement to traditional arbitration.
(3) Other kinds of mediation, including mediation offered by law firms and others on a purely private basis.

Irrespective of the kind of mediation that is used, the parties must agree to participate; otherwise, mediation has no meaning.

314. However, mediation clauses in arbitral agreements in modern contracts often 'oblige' parties to instigate mediation, but if it is clear that a party can or will not participate, the arbitral case can be instigated without further delay. Often, the mediation clause allows the parties a certain portion of time, e.g., six weeks, to reach a result through mediation, and if a result is not reached, each party can instigate arbitration. There will always be an exception in the clause, stating that if the matter is urgent, the six-week period does not have to be respected.

Chapter 2. Rights That Can Be Subject to Mediation

315. Such matters must be defined in the same way as the rights that can be subject to arbitration, i.e., matters on which the parties can make an agreement.

Chapter 3. Mediation Agreement

316. The agreement can either be contained in a contract, often as part of an arbitration clause. Or the mediation agreement can be made in a rather informal way when a case has been instigated before a court, and the court, or one of the parties, suggests that this case is suitable for court mediation.

Chapter 4. Persons/Institutions That Can Act as Mediator

317. If court mediation takes place, the mediator will be one of the persons appointed by the court as mediator. A number of advocates and judges have shown interest for this, and they have all been educated as mediators. In the individual case, the court appoints one of the trained educators from the list.

318. If mediation takes place privately, or under an institution, such as Danish Arbitration (Voldgiftsinstituttet), an arbitrator is suggested by the institute, and the arbitrator must be accepted by both parties.

Chapter 5. Mediation Procedure

319. A mediation under Danish Arbitration (Voldgiftsinstituttet) will often follow these steps: (1) introduction and setting the framework, (2) statements and summaries, (3) private meetings (so-called caucus), (4) settlement agreement and completion.

Chapter 6. Settlement Agreement

320. The settlement agreement does in principle not differ from other civil agreements. The agreement is not dependent on recognition by the court.

Chapter 7. Setting Aside a Settlement Agreement

321. The settlement agreement is subject to being set aside in the same way and to the same extent as other agreements. There are no specific provisions on settlement agreements.

Chapter 8. International Mediation

322. International mediation, being it court mediation or private mediation, does not differ from the mediation mentioned above, which is common for all types of mediation, no matter whether it is purely domestic, or it is cross-border.

Selected Bibliography

Bang-Pedersen, Ulrik Rammeskow & Lasse Højlund Christensen. *Den civile retspleje*. 2nd ed. Gyldendal, 2011.

Gomard, Bernhard & Michael Kistrup. *Civilprocessen*. 8th ed. Karnov Group, 2020.

Gomard, Bernhard, et al. (eds). *Retsplejeloven med kommentarer*. 10th ed. 2018.

Hertz, Ketilbjørn. *Bruxelles I-forordningen med kommentarer*. 2nd ed. DJØF Forlag, 2015.

Juul, Jakob & Peter Fauerholdt Thommesen. *Voldgiftsret*. 3rd ed. Karnov Group, 2017.

Petersen, Lars Lindencrone & Erik Werlauff. *Dansk retspleje*. 8th ed. Karnov Group, 2020.

Selected Bibliography

Index

The numbers here refer to paragraph numbers.

Index

Index

Index

www.ingramcontent.com/pod-product-compliance
Lightning Source LLC
Chambersburg PA
CBHW071340230926
51846CB00002B/396
9789403501963